Fabulous

F WORDS

OF

BUSINESS OWNERSHIP

Redefining Choice Words
To Fuel Your Small Business

FABI W. PRESLAR

SPARK Publications
Charlotte, North Carolina

Fabulous F Words of Business Ownership:
Redefining Choice Words to Fuel Your Small Business
Fabi W. Preslar

Designed, edited, produced, and published by
SPARK Publications
SPARKpublications.com
Charlotte, NC

Printed in the United States of America
Paperback, October 2018, ISBN: 978-1-943070-39-8
E-book, October 2018, ISBN: 978-1-943070-40-4
Audio book, December 2018
Library of Congress Control Number: 2018957899

BUSINESS & ECONOMICS / Small Business
BIOGRAPHY & AUTOBIOGRAPHY / Business
SELF-HELP / Personal Growth / Success

Fabulous F WORDS OF BUSINESS OWNERSHIP ™

This book is dedicated to
Jean Pierre and Jacqueline, my parents,
who set me on the journey to a beautiful life
and the path to business ownership.

And to Larry and Sofi who are my reasons to succeed.

"Fabi's vulnerability and authentic sharing shines brightly in how she sheds a light of her lessons learned through her twenty-year journey of business ownership. Whether you have just started a business or are in the throes of chaos in an existing one, *Fabulous F Words of Business Ownership* will give you clues, insights, and the validation necessary to forge forward with a true sense that you are never in this journey alone." – Sherré D.

"Fabi creates accessibility through her vulnerability, making it easy to draw parallels between her business journey and my own. No matter where you are on your path, through both her hard lessons and sparkly successes, you'll find relatable nuggets that will make you nod, make you think, and most of all, speak deeply to you on a level that only a fellow entrepreneur can." – Chrystal R.

"There are two sides to every business: the analytical, and the emotional. This book weaves those two sides seamlessly together into an educational, enjoyable, and fun journey. Part 'what not to do in business' and part 'what I wish I'd known about the human element of running a business,' this book entertains and gets real at the same time—often in the same sentence. I'm walking away with new insights into how I run my business, mistakes to avoid in the future, a renewed clarity around lessons I've learned from my past failures, and the truth about fear, failure, and fortunes as a small business owner!" – Julie B.

"Fabi never quits. Like all business owners, she learns every day and challenges herself to make her business better. If you're thinking of throwing in the towel, read this book and think again. Pick yourself up and get to work growing your company, but don't forget what you've learned along the way." – Matt B.

"Fabi offers us insight into her thoughts, vulnerabilities, and fears as she has grown in her understanding of herself and her role as a leader in her business, her family, and her community. Fabi's writing style is conversational. You will feel as if she is in the room talking to you. I recommend that you read the book on a day when you can finish it entirely. You won't want to put it down." – Debbie P.

"I wish I'd read this sooner as I see mistakes I am currently making in my business ownership. I also am going to reread important chapters, so these lessons truly sink in. *The Fabulous F Words of Business Ownership* is a must-read for women who are serious about making their businesses successful. Fabi Preslar has pointed out roadblocks to avoid in this entertaining, fast-reading, insightful book. She is heartbreakingly honest and incredibly smart. Rush to get this book!" – Kim B.

"This book is a fabulous guideline for the dos, the don't dos, and the potential pitfalls of business ownership. Fabi's non-sugarcoated look at her own experience is encouraging and often humorous. Her open sharing of her downfalls as well as her successes in a down-to-earth, conversational style will inspire others to continue when they might think they have to give up and abandon their dreams. This book presented questions to ask myself and ideas that I had not previously considered in my daily life." – Melody M.

"The book is a marriage of what it is to be a business owner and a human being at the same time. Great lessons on the ins and outs of life. I loved it!" – Anne L.

"When choosing a good book with which you can grow both personally and professionally, *Fabulous F Words of Business Ownership* is a power-packed read that will fill you with faith and fortitude to finish what you started." – Christopher D.

Table of Contents

Owning a business is chock-full of *F* words and is not for the faint of heart.

Foreshadow

An Introduction to *F* Words

What does the letter *F* at the top of a page say to you? Does it scream "failure" and symbolize imperfection, weakness, and struggle? If so, you're not alone.

Launching, growing, and running a small business is not for the faint of heart. It is a roller-coaster ride with wicked ups and downs and loops that can make you queasy or outright sick. There's always a risk that everything you've built may become permanently derailed. But let's face it: we business owners are not merry-go-round types.

Plenty of awesome books and programs teach strategies and processes to successfully conquer each step of your business. This is not *that* book. It is not a how-to book, nor is it a workbook, although there is room for reflection. This is a book about a small business ownership journey toward success by redefining failure, identifying doubts and fears, and infusing love and spirituality into your business. Although the sentiment of the most famous four-letter *F* word is shared in anecdotes, I've omitted the actual word because there are so many more meaningful replacements. A dictionary's worth of *F* words have marked my business journey and provided me with valuable insights and lessons along the way.

This is a collection of lessons earned and learned from my business ownership ride. It is written from an introvert's perspective; however, the lessons can benefit extroverts as well. It includes examples of how I faced and challenged my personal beliefs and the impact that family history has had on my business decisions. I've made a great many mistakes and gathered knowledge the hard way.

As my business has grown, I've grown as a person. And with every step, whether that step was forward or backward, I've gained spiritual insights and strengthened my business knowledge.

First up: "family" and "finances." My French parents brought me into this world as an *F* word—Fabienne—which worked fine as my family moved around the world. When we moved to the Carolinas, my lovely, lyrical name became a drawled out "Fabi-Anne." I cut my name in half and became Fabi. (For the record, it's pronounced "Faybee.") I communicate a great deal via email, and when I eventually introduce myself in person or over the phone, I'm often greeted with, "Oh, I thought you were a dude." I'm not.

Though far from financially wealthy, my family was highly inventive and self-sufficient and, for reasons I didn't understand at the time, seemed frequently filled with fear. Despite the challenges, this upbringing served me well. I've been able to build a rich life and a strong livelihood by being creative, resourceful, and resilient. My foundation (another *F* word) has been longevity and love.

My business has been at the core of every difficult lesson learned. Many times I've wanted to "*F* it all" and do something easier than run a business. But there's that longevity thing and that voice—oh, that voice—from within. And as I learn more about myself, the voice grows louder. It's intent on me creating things I know I'm not yet capable of creating. Yet somehow I do, and in the process I've occasionally felt like a fraud.

Much of my success in business has come from being open and vulnerable. This kind of transparency creates challenges too, but for the most part, it attracts other kind, helpful, successful, vulnerable people. If you've picked up this book, I suspect at least a few of those traits apply to you as well.

My hope is that this book will help you redefine a few choice words to fuel your small business. By the last chapter, my desire is that you will have gained new tools to better network, build your culture, break through any doubt, and nurture your business with love and wisdom.

Launching, growing, and *running* a *small business* is not for the faint of heart. It is a *roller-coaster ride* with *wicked ups* and *downs* and *loops* that can make you *queasy* or *outright sick*. There's always a risk that everything you've built may become *permanently* derailed. But let's face it: *we business owners are not merry-go-round types.*

Your family history brings a great deal into your business and how you will interact with your employees and build your team. Take time to understand these subconscious defaults and how they can help or hurt your business.

CHAPTER 1

Foundations

Entrepreneurship in the Genes

A lifetime of experiences has shaped each of us and created a foundation of beliefs and attitudes that stand at the core of our decisions. What that foundation is built on is different for everyone. How it affects our businesses depends on how we build on it (or not) and how sturdy and true it stands.

I've spent the last few years removing old foundation pieces that no longer support my life. It isn't easy to replace, remove, and rebuild a foundation, but just as we eventually realize the truth about Santa Claus and the boogeyman, so go old beliefs about our capabilities, other people, love, fear, money, and so on. We owe it to ourselves to examine our foundations to find the strong points and the cracks and update and upgrade as necessary.

Here's how my foundation was formed. Both of my parents were born in France into large families whose lives were entrenched in fear and scarcity at the end of World War II. Shortly after they married, they expressed their newfound freedom by moving to the Montreal, Canada area, where I was born. The three of us then moved to the Bahamas, where we lived for three years. My mom and I also lived in Paris for about nine months, and there my sister was born. From there we immigrated to the States via Florida and worked our way up the East Coast, finally landing in the Carolinas. My parents kept their beautiful French accents, while my sister and I sound like homegrown Southern women.

My introduction to entrepreneurship came from watching my dad conduct his many interesting side businesses as a serial entrepreneur. He was often chasing the lure of "the big money" as he described it—raising chinchillas in the heat of Florida, for instance. (I never wanted to know why and to this day still haven't asked.) There was also the occasional multilevel marketing business. Or his mail-order program for people who wanted to flatten their big bellies. Customers mailed a SASE (self-addressed stamped envelope) and a dollar to our home address, and he'd mail back a set of illustrated exercise instructions (he's a very talented artist). This was the equivalent of today's lead generation techniques. Then there was the business repairing vinyl car seats, chair cushions, and pleather jackets, among other things. He ran that operation for about a year as he worked tirelessly at launching his own restaurant.

Along with his salaried jobs and his side jobs he maintained a small but abundant organic farm. That farm provided our vegetables, meat, eggs, and milk for many years. There were also other ventures, such as raising Afghan hounds, making leather accessories, and creating log carvings.

Mom provided us with homemade bread, yogurt, and dried fruits. She tended a hydroponic garden of nutritious sprouts inside our home. Mom worked at several restaurants, and when my parents opened their restaurant, she worked long hours there. Small business ownership often requires a total family commitment, whether its members voluntarily commit to it or not.

Eating organic foods and bringing sandwiches made with homemade whole-wheat bread and sprouts to school for lunch would be fairly cool and mainstream now. But this was decades before the farm-to-table movement, and during the late '70s in rural South Carolina, it was far, far from cool. It was just plain weird. My sister and I were harassed daily and perceived as odd foreigners. All this homegrown food not only made us grow healthy and tall but also helped us grow thick skins that toughened us up for the future.

By today's standards, that organic lifestyle is for those who have accomplished a level of financial freedom. For my parents, it had more to do with providing food for the family because, despite my parents' paying jobs, there was little money coming in. My parents spent all their time and energy working very hard to make very little money. I remember the many wishes and hopes I had for a second pair of shoes or a pair of jeans that would cover my anklebones. High-water bellbottoms from Kmart on a five-foot, ten-inch, fifteen-year-old girl were not the makings of popularity. Money was always scarce or very tight. Tensions ran tight throughout my family as well.

Although my parents did the absolute best they could within a culture they did not know well and with what they knew about life itself, they rarely shared affection. While there was a great deal of creativity and work ethic, there was also a huge amount of friction and rigidity. I never lacked for the absolute basics of life. Still, I craved more, but at such a young age, I did not know what to ask for or how to do it.

As I positively reframe this lifestyle in today's language, I realize that my parents practiced sustainable innovation. They instilled in me a model for thinking for myself, employing self-sustaining methods, working long, hard hours, and creating a life of freedom. I've carried that creativity, fierce sense of independence, and uncompromising work ethic into my adult life and my own business. However, I also carried a deep sense of lack and doubt and the belief that I had to figure things out by myself. I had no sense that other folks could provide affection as part of daily life. I self-protected by creating a tough outer shell that covered a deeply introverted and fear-filled young lady. I'll share more about that in later chapters, but know that chipping away at that shell has helped my business and me to grow.

Losing Everything

When I was fifteen years old, my dad opened his first physical business, a restaurant in Columbia, South Carolina, which was about forty minutes from our self-sufficient farm and home. He was a creative chef who was ahead of his time, but he didn't have the skills needed to run that type of business.

The summer before my senior year of high school, our world came tumbling down. We lost the restaurant, our farm, our home, and the livelihood we knew. Yvonne, a family friend near Winston-Salem, North Carolina, opened her home to my family. What kind of angel would take in a family of two beaten-down adults and two angry teenage girls who didn't have a clue about the real world?

My fear transformed into self-survival, anger, and a desire to reinvent myself. I didn't understand why we were leaving our home and the life we knew; I was simply told we were moving.

From this, I learned the value of transparency. I've applied this lesson as a parent to my daughter, and I've also brought this transparency into my business. I feel sure that she and my employees would sometimes prefer I not be as transparent as I am, but it's important that those I love and lead are aware of, at least to some degree, whatever situation we're in at the moment.

Deep within my dad's own foundational beliefs was the notion that the man of the house shouldn't discuss hardship; he just had to do what was right for his family's survival. It wasn't until I began writing this book that we ever discussed this critical period of my family's life. His perspective revealed so much about so many things. Even more, it showed me how he did what he knew to do based on his family programming and foundational beliefs. Having this exchange with him

Small business
ownership often
requires a total
family commitment,
whether its members
voluntarily
commit to it
or not.

helped me to chip away at a few more antiquated pieces of my personal foundation.

Stepping Out on My Own

At age seventeen, in the same month I graduated from high school, I left home. I had an aching desire to get my adult life started, and I set out to do it with a blank rule book. At my request, my mother dropped me off at an all-girls dorm for transient girls in Charlotte, North Carolina. I had no money, no car, and the little that I owned fit in her small car. I knew no one. I was alone and ready to launch my own life.

I filed for US citizenship and enrolled in Central Piedmont Community College to become a graphic designer. Between a Pell Grant, student loan, work-study program, and working two additional jobs, I managed to pay for my own livelihood and education. I lived in that dorm with sixty (yes 60) other girls for two years—that alone was some real-world, fast-tracked education.

For the first twenty-two years of my career, no one knew about my entry to Charlotte, and no one knew that my formal education maxed out with a two-year community college associate's degree in graphic design. I was busy creating the next great version of myself while building on top of a foundation made of some wobbly stones.

I buried my past for a long time. I wanted to protect myself from the pain and fear of being unfairly judged by others.

That all changed the day I gave a presentation to a group of about seventy professionals, many of whom had inspired me at some point during my career. They'd come to celebrate a fun, promotional award with me. But as I stood at the podium to accept it, I somehow knew that the story of my business journey wasn't the one this crowd needed to hear. They'd all taught me so much, and I felt compelled to share another story—the story of my personal journey. After all, my story is part of my company's story. Sharing your story out loud, especially if it's the first time, feels like stripping down. Personally, I felt as if I'd somehow cracked my carefully preserved personal foundation.

The response afterward was overwhelming. Many colleagues mistakenly assumed that I came from a wealthy upbringing and that I'd been simply handed my own successful publications firm. All the effort to improve myself and all the polish I'd applied to my business had been misinterpreted. Folks told me how they had filled in the gaps of what they knew about me, mostly with tales of wealth and a luxury life in France. As the adage goes, in the absence of information, people make stuff up. In many cases, those made-up facts don't help anyone. In this particular case, the realness of where I came from was missing. Knowing my humble background made me more approachable in their eyes. A number of people expressed that they were inspired by my personal story. If I could transform my life, then they could too.

This was the nudge I needed to write my story, which I did in my first book, *On Heaven's Couch: A Journey with a Masterful Mentor*. It detailed my experiences with Yvonne, the friend who took my family in when I was a teenager and who served as my life-long guide and mentor.

I must admit that I've grown a little tired of telling "my story." It's the foundation of who I've become, but it is not who I am. Today the focus is on a new story—the one that has no ending yet. I understand and treasure the path my past has put in front of me. I no longer pretend to know the specific path my journey may take. What I do know is that it's wise to create a basic roadmap, and whatever pops up on that path is part of the experience and lesson I need to go through to gain access to my next experience and lesson.

I felt the itch to write this second book in the midst of another foundation rattling series of failures, seven years to the week that I committed to writing my first book.

Fascinating.

Failing Forefathers

The complete failure of my dad's biggest leap in business ownership was a crushing experience. It left a wound I wanted to heal for my family and for myself. I've always believed that desire fueled my business journey.

But still, alongside the deep-in-my-bones need to succeed as a business owner was a paralyzing fear of failure at every step. I'd always assumed the fear reflected my own insecurity or lack of skills. It seemed that no matter how hard I tried to move forward, I repeatedly smacked into a wall of fear, which shot me backward in my journey. In the middle of writing this book, an amazing piece of family history was revealed to me.

My beloved French aunt made a rare visit to the States. We were sitting outside on my deck, which is surrounded by dozens of 100-foot-tall trees. It's my favorite place in the world.

We were reminiscing, and my aunt began talking about how much my family in France hurt for my parents, my sister, and me all those years ago when we lost the restaurant, our way of life, and our home. It pained my aunts and grandmother across the ocean that my sister and I, two young teenage girls at the time, were pulled away from all we knew to live with another family in a different state.

And then she said, "Especially because your father knew what his grandfather had gone through."

I felt the whooshing sensation of being pulled backward. "Wait, what did you say?" I asked.

"Didn't you know your great-grandfather was an entrepreneur and owned a business?"

I hadn't. Apparently, in the mid-1920s, my great-grandfather on my father's side launched and owned Wilmart Bank. He and my great-grandmother were *very* wealthy and lived on Ile St. Louis in Paris, France, a traditional refuge of the Parisian upper class. It was one of two islands in the middle of Paris, the other being Ile de la Cité, home to Notre Dame de Paris. The couple had many servants and enjoyed the kind of

Roaring Twenties lifestyle only the elite could afford. My great-grandmother was quite a socialite and hosted and attended glamorous events and parties.

The economic crash in October 1929 marked the beginning of my family's descent into extreme poverty. The crash wiped out the bank and damaged the finances of its patrons. My great-grandfather had such a deep sense of responsibility for his clients (whether out of goodness or guilt, we will never know) that he sold all of his possessions and assets. Everything he and his family owned was sold to help repay his clients' losses. It's been said that the great loss of his business caused him unbearable stress and heartbreak and brought about his early death. This left my great-grandmother destitute with two young boys. She was left to live in the attic maid quarters of one of the buildings they used to own, where she mended clothes by hand for mere francs. This former socialite could barely afford food to keep herself and her two boys alive. Details are vague, since neither she nor her sons spoke about this part of the family history.

As I listened to my aunt tell me this never-before-mentioned story, I experienced the feeling of going back through time. It was like watching a movie of my great-grandparents' life. I could feel my great-grandmother's pain of going from riches to rags and her determination to survive. My great-grandmother became innovative and industrious to care for her sons. My emotions while hearing this story were a visceral pressure on my chest and an ache in my stomach. I felt and saw everything my aunt was revealing to me about my ancestors. Her story answered so many questions while planting seeds for so many more.

I thought briefly about conducting research on my ancestors' history but decided that the factual details were not important to me. It's no wonder I've always felt I had something I needed to redeem. Mixed with the heavy feeling of this story was also a wave of understanding and clarity, of relief and responsibility. What *is* important is the imprint and impact the story has left on my family and me. I don't need evidence of the story's validity; the reaction in my body was proof that it held truth within me.

I'm quite convinced that events in our family lineage get stored in our cells, or maybe they're housed in a spiritual archive and passed along through generations of family values. Either way, our heritage can directly impact our paths of least resistance—how we think, how we act, how we react, what sort of businesses we launch, how we hire and manage employees—the list goes on. Some business owners succeed with those defaults intact. But I'd wager many more of us find greater success when we examine our pasts to proactively determine what we choose to carry with us into the future.

Living On

I never knew my grandfather well, but others describe him as a guarded, rigid, and cautious man. Of course, as his first grandchild, I remember him as all hugs.

He was adamant that his four children (my father, aunts, and uncle) receive a solid education and get steady jobs. He wanted security for his children and their families. No wonder he was angry at my father for being an artist and a chef and for learning a trade instead of going to university. But in those days, a man was not inclined to talk about his personal fears. My grandfather expressed them instead as anger, shame, and disappointment.

I can only imagine the subconscious fears that ran rampant through my father's family. Those same deep fears were passed on to me, but they did not stay buried. They've risen to the surface, screaming to be redeemed.

If I'd known this information many years sooner, I might not have beat myself up so harshly or felt restricted at every step by shackles of fear. Then again, had it been revealed earlier in my life, I may not have had the courage to start my company to begin with. If generations of my forefathers couldn't succeed, what would make me think I could?

So maybe learning this now, as I'm reflecting on my business journey at this later-in-life stage, is perfect spiritual timing. It allows me to pass along the lesson I've learned—that our family histories live on in the way we think about business ownership and the decisions it entails.

Full Circle: Framing Your Story

What kind of family history do you bring into your business?

How does your past strengthen your business?

In what ways does your family history complicate the way you approach business decisions?

Sometimes your own ego holds you back. Framing the situation with the right questions offers a way around your internal barriers.

CHAPTER 2

Framing

Perspective without Ego

"Ego" seems to mean lots of different things to different people. So when I refer to "ego," note that I'm talking about the part of the brain that carries out our programmed way of protecting ourselves. Also note the keyword "programmed." Our programs were written early in our lives by our parents, grandparents, teachers, and society. Then we added on to them with a mix of intention, knowledge, and a sprinkle of dreams and purpose. Now that program runs efficiently in the background, usually without our awareness even though it impacts nearly every decision we make.

The ego can be tremendously helpful when, for example, it stokes feelings of resilience and courage to help us guide our businesses through tough times. Or it can make us our own worst enemies when, for example, it stokes our fears of taking the wrong step, so we miss valuable opportunities. In such times, an ego adjustment is necessary.

Ego Adjustment

I'm extremely sensitive; I was born with a soft, squishy core. I know this about myself. However, growing up with a lack of love, a lack of resources, and an abundance of emotion made me develop a tough outer shell. My ego was programmed to protect me by being strong.

When I moved away from home at age seventeen—alone with no money in a city where I knew no one—I had to take care of myself because there was no one else. During those tough times, a huge amount of internal programming (and pouring more concrete onto a shaky foundation) took place. My ego grew. I became so internally focused and consumed with protecting myself that it was impossible to accept help from anyone. They'd just let me down anyway, right?

As I launched my career and encountered rejection, disappointment, sabotage, and selfishness, that outer shell got thicker and thicker. As my outer shell continued to grow so did my ego, to keep me strong and safe.

Recently I've learned to see my protective e-g-o, as many have noted, as an acronym for "edging God out." What a clear and accurate description for that overly protective ego. Along with shielding me from any "bad," my outer shell kept out any good that might otherwise enter.

Running a business, leading, innovating, and sharing the value of our companies does require a healthy ego. I've also seen some beautifully spiritual business owners who weren't tapped into the healthy parts of their egos, so they took no action. They waited for things to come to their businesses. That can be a very long and very slow journey, if you move at all. Action is required. And often multiple simultaneous actions are needed.

The Right Questions

That's where asking great questions comes in. Questions create a secret path around your ego and programming. Here's another way of looking at it: questions are like picture frames that help you put problems on the wall and study them from a new perspective, one that doesn't get your ego in a tizzy.

I'm constantly checking in with myself and asking myself questions. I often go on a quest for the perfect question. Identifying the right question provides the answers I need to understand, strengthen, or alter my direction. Searching for the answer itself rarely serves me well. That answer may in fact put me on the wrong path. Think about it. If I go seeking answers, I may select what I subconsciously want the answer to be, the one that validates my programming, not necessarily the correct answer.

Once I wondered whether the employee I was interviewing was the right one and decided to look for the answer in the form of a sign. I noticed that her license plate numbers contained my birthdate. Wow, how often does that happen? It must be a sign that I should hire her, right? After all, none of the other candidates had my birthdate on their license plates.

I know you're probably laughing at me, but at the time I believed this was a sign that she was "the one." Well, she was the one all right. That employee taught me all sorts of painful lessons, and the situation didn't end well. Still, the experience helped me to understand that I tend to see what I want to see. And I learned that if I look for a question instead of a sign, I'll find an answer that's a better fit.

My business reveals answers on a daily basis. Asking a targeted question when there are so many potential answers is powerful.

One of my favorite questions is from Theodore Levitt and Peter Drucker: "What business am I in?" When I'm assessing my firm's profitability or determining whether we've gotten too fragmented, I need to be able to answer this question with a single short sentence. This is an entirely different question than, are we making money? The answer often puts a screeching halt to accepting clients or projects that aren't a fit.

Another go-to set of questions: What's the worst that could happen? What's the best that could happen? What actually happens is usually somewhere in the middle.

I hope you can see the importance of finding the right question. Business ownership is an amazing ego adjuster; one way or another, you'll find the right level of ego for your journey and your business needs.

If you are struggling to reveal the right questions to ask yourself, perhaps your first question then becomes, who can help me with this issue? And that may be the very question you use to begin searching for a mentor or a valuable guide.

Full Circle: Framing Your Story

In what ways is your ego
holding you back?

What is your ego trying
to protect you from?

What frame can you put
around an issue to help
your ego see it differently?

Questions are like
picture frames that help
you put *problems* on
the wall and *study* them
from a *new perspective*,
one that doesn't
get your
ego in a tizzy.

When you are ready, your guide will appear. Use their counsel and questions to foresee needs now and in the future.

CHAPTER 3

Foresight

Getting Clearer with Guides

Business owners usually aren't followers; I'm not. So we need guides who, instead of telling us what to do, teach us to ask the right questions. Mine are also good at knowing exactly how to stir up my inner "stuff." These guides help me with questions that provide great foresight into a predicament I'm in or possibly creating.

My experiences have confirmed that when the student is ready, the guide appears. Each time I came to a precipice in my life, I asked the Universe for help (the Universe as in God, the 'Verse, the Heavens, the Powers that Be, or whatever else you choose to call it). Sometimes help came as a guide carrying a quick message. Or a book that fell off the shelf and dropped open to the exact words I needed to read. Or an email with someone's blog post that pointed out a question I needed to ask.

Asking for help taps into our vulnerability and courage. It also lets the ego know that we know that we don't know everything. You know? It asks that we drop our shields just a little and trust that someone else may have the wisdom we need to move forward.

When I reached a point in my young life at which I could accept help and was open to new perspectives, my first guide appeared. I want to share a little about my experiences with my guides, both to show you the impact they have had on my business and on me and to honor them. My greatest wish for you is that you find equally amazing guides.

Yvonne

Yvonne, a dear family friend, was a vibrant, wise, and energetic woman. She was one of those teachers who never sought out students. Yet when I made a silent cry for help, I was drawn to her. Yvonne was a beacon in my life over many years—a beacon of truth, love, and service.

Yvonne's and my story has parallels to *Tuesdays with Morrie*. Like Morrie, my mentor became gravely ill. I'd just launched my business when I learned that she'd become physically disabled and in need of full-time care. I let Yvonne know that I'd be available to her every Monday and occasional weekends for as long as she needed me. I made that weekly, four-hour round trip to Yvonne's home for ten years. And with each visit, I grew closer to her. My "Mondays with Yvonne" were life changing.

As hard as it was to get away from my life and make that drive, her home was a haven for me. It was a place of truth, beauty, and service. Yvonne's mobility within her house was severely limited. Her life was reduced to the space within an arm's reach from where she sat on her couch. There were plenty of chores to complete for Yvonne—organizing her medications and vitamins for the week, applying lotions to soothe her neuropathy, washing her laundry, mopping her floors, entertaining the dog, cooking breakfast, and cleaning the cat box. I usually worked on these household chores in between our conversations.

Conversations with Yvonne were sometimes difficult and often humbling. My focus each week was to listen and learn as

I sat next to her on the couch. She always asked me to share my interpretations of what had happened in my life during the previous week. She asked tough questions and imparted great wisdom.

Carlos

Yvonne's death left a great void in my life. I missed her deep, probing questions and the mirroring feedback she provided. I began a search for my next guide, but I wasn't impressed by the various professionals I spoke with. To be fair, my next guide would have some big shoes to fill.

My dear friend, speaking coach, and client, Lou, invited me to attend an event she was hosting. At this event, Carlos, a dynamic and creative Argentinian man, stepped up to speak. As he shared his transformational story and his clients' breakthroughs, the top of my head began to tingle uncontrollably, like there was a hive of bees dancing on top of my brain. I knew he was my next guide.

What I didn't know was how to make it happen. It took courage to let him know my intentions. Carlos works his insightful breakthrough and peak performance magic with Swiss bankers, global executives, high-level innovators, world-class and Olympic athletes, and me. He made it happen.

Carlos and I remain friends and collaborators. He still squeezes me into his schedule of world travels for an occasional breakthrough power-boost conversation. Carlos has inspired me to continue pushing my boundaries in business and taught me how to manage my energy instead of my time.

Each of us hosts events designed to fuel our personal need for insightful conversation and creative collaboration. We attend each other's events and have grown our respective networks. My professional network will never match his super-influential global network, but if I ever needed to meet one of his contacts, I feel sure I'd receive a warm connection.

While Yvonne paved the way for me to become a productive, loving, and caring adult, Carlos showed me the path to breakthrough to whatever "moon-shot" business goal I had.

Mike

I'm a tough case for anyone who accepts the challenge of acting as my guide. None have been challenged more than Mike.

Before I met him, I'd become physically sick with migraines and issues with several organs. I'd had two major, life-changing surgeries within nine months, and each of those surgeries had complications.

After many months of healing, I thought all was well. Then another crazy pain started in my lower left abdomen. I had a general visit scheduled with my hormone doctor and shared my symptoms. She gave me her horrifying opinion and recommended surgery. I left her office literally running, on the verge of an emotional breakdown.

Another surgery? What was I missing? I'd learned so much during this healing process. What was I not seeing about myself? What life lessons was I not understanding?

I was ready to scream out loud in frustration when my mobile phone rang. It was my best friend, Carla. She'd had a feeling something was up with me and wanted to check in. (We both get that weird message-y feeling about one other on occasion.) I cried out my story to her. Carla calmed me down and urged me to get a second opinion.

The next morning a second doctor confirmed I needed to go back into surgery.

Every single part of my body was pissed off. I felt like I had failed my broken-down body and had no tools, no knowledge left. I was dumbfounded.

Asking for help
taps into
our *vulnerability*
and *courage.*
It also lets the ego
know that *we know* that we
don't know everything.
You know?

On the ride back from the doctor, I was listening to an audiobook by Wayne Dyer. He talked about CST (craniosacral therapy) and how this technique can help release the trauma within a person's cells. There's an entire science about cell memory. I had not heard of such a thing. Could this be the missing link in my recovery?

Quickly I began to research the topic online, looking for experts in this field of study. What does cell memory do physically to the body? How is this trauma released?

I was seeking someone who understood, believed, and could discuss this "cells hold trauma" notion with me. Amazingly, I found a practitioner named Mike who wasn't hours away but only four miles from my office!

We met, and I shared my journey. After fifteen minutes he asked me, "Why are you here?" I answered that I was seeking the question I didn't know to ask.

I honestly feel I was led to Mike in the same way I was led to Yvonne and Carlos. Mike became a trusted guide.

CST was not the answer for me, but it was the entry into finding the guide who could help me frame the questions I needed to ask for the answers I was seeking. I now have a new toolbox that I've been able to access to think bigger thoughts. And help heal my body.

Mike mirrored my responses, helped me explore new perspectives, and turned those insights into great questions. I've discovered a new level of self-confidence and greater creativity, which helped me transition and further grow my business.

Oh, and there's more to this story. I'd let my doctor know that I'd decided to heal using integrative healing practices. She was very concerned when I cancelled the surgery. However, my ultrasound at an annual follow-up exam revealed medical evidence that surgery was no longer necessary.

I believe this process was a gift from my body to learn some deep lessons. I gained fresh knowledge, a healthy body, and new, more purpose-driven goals.

So what's all this got to do with business?

For me, everything. The success and the well-being of a small business is directly tied to the health and mindset of its owner. If our thoughts and health are not at peak performance, our businesses reflect it. And when we are operating at peak performance, our businesses reflect that too.

So you see, it *is* all about me. And, of course, it's all about you! Having a wise guide to help you find the right questions is invaluable.

Larry

Last, but by no means least, is my forever guide, Larry. Larry is my dear husband and partner in all aspects of my life. He is my guide above all guides, providing stability, challenging me beyond what I think my capabilities are, and encouraging me to reach new heights. He's also a gem for understanding (to a degree, anyway) why I've needed these guides over our many years together.

How I have been blessed with this degree of support is one of the mysteries of my life. Early in our relationship, I took Larry for granted, not believing that this level of love was even possible for me. As we've grown together, our relationship has been, and continues to be, the most precious component of my life. There are simply no words to do it justice.

Tapping into the 'Verse

Having these guides has been of great value to my personal journey, my business trajectory, and to the dismantling and rebuilding of my personal foundation. The times I go without having a regularly scheduled guide are often great times of "doing." When it is time again to ponder another journey, I feel confident the right guide will appear at the right time with the right message.

Of course, your journey and the right guides may be completely different than mine. Our journeys' foundations, our knowledge, and our passions are different, and the way we react to everything around us can be different. But I've learned that reinventing the wheel is a terrible business model. There is nothing so special about me or my business that I can't adapt and learn from someone else. So let's go innovate, but let's not reinvent something that we don't need to. Let's tap into the knowledge of the 'Verse," the "web," and the people who've already been there, done that. For me, a specialized guide has been of extreme value in helping me to better see what's needed now and in the future.

Full Circle: Framing Your Story

Who have been
your personal and
business guides?

If you could have a guide
today, what would they
guide you through?

What process will you
now go through to
attract your guide?

The *success* and
the *well-being*
of a small business
is *directly tied* to the
health *and* mindset
of its owner.

Foraging for information has never been easier, but it has limits. Invest in some formal education on running a business, especially if your regular degree didn't cover everything from financial modeling to employment contracts.

CHAPTER 4

Foraging

You Don't Know What You Don't Know

My dad's first business success came after I'd already left home. As a chef and an artist, he has many skills that come easily to him. He created a how-to book so that others could make the unique, decorative food carvings and garnishes he's delighted so many folks with over the years. He produced all the illustrations and step-by-step instructions. I typeset and completed the page layout for the book. Through his own promotional efforts, he received orders from schools, hospitals, nursing homes, and restaurants. He partnered with another chef and sold several thousand books. He also spoke at workshops, seminars, and food shows. I attended a couple of my father's presentations. His humor, charm, and talent—packaged perfectly with a French accent—were always crowd pleasers.

A highlight for him was the opportunity to speak to over forty college professors during a homecoming event at a college in Raleigh, North Carolina. Dad had never received a college degree in the States, and by US standards he didn't even have the equivalent of a GED. Yet here he was, invited to teach a practical art form to a group of professors.

I can relate.

There was never an emphasis on education in my family. My parents believed that hard work and developed talent were all that was needed to survive. When I graduated, I had an associate's degree in graphic design. I quickly discovered that my two-year hard-earned degree often wasn't enough to get me an interview for the countless jobs for which I'd applied. It did, however, create a great foundation to become a creative designer.

A graphic design position was open at a large, local university. I knew I could do the work described, but I was told that without a four-year bachelor's degree, I couldn't be considered. Years later, without further formal education, I was a guest speaker at two events for students and community guests at that same university. I also responded to a statewide request for proposal (RFP) to produce some of that school's ongoing graphic design projects. After rounds of proposals, interviews, and reviews of our work, my firm won the five-year university account. I felt, firsthand, that sideways feeling of accomplishment that my dad experienced. Not only did it feel great, but also it confirmed how far skill and hard work had taken me.

Hard Knocks University, School of Life, or whatever you wish to call it, non-formal education isn't easy. It's hit or miss, and you don't know what you don't know, so there's nothing to research. That's why we must constantly be open and on the lookout for new information and opportunities to learn. That said, not all sources are created equal.

Doing Better by Knowing Better

If you're going to start or own a business, it's best to know the basics. Learn realistic guidelines and expectations from a legal, tax, property, license, and ethics standpoint. Information about business plans, marketing plans, and business models are readily available.

I bootstrapped six years in my first business and eighteen years in my second business with hard-knock, life-university knowledge. I foraged through countless seminars, workshops, and webinars, gathering knowledge on running a business, marketing, accounting, finances, building a team, building a culture, and becoming a leader. Name the class, and I've probably attended it.

In hindsight, I realize that I seldom researched the credibility of these programs. The content was basic, and many of these classes offered only a small amount of information, serving primarily as lead-generation efforts for the presenters.

Picking up a nugget of information here and there isn't a bad thing, yet it is a slow, unreliable way to learn. Until I received the learning opportunity of a lifetime, though, I didn't see how my bootstrapped, self-education process was actually holding my business back and delaying needed progress. Mentally going back in time won't change this; however, reflecting on this process and the many stronger options available will hopefully help you seek a much more reliable process for learning the critical aspects of your business.

Fire Hose of Knowledge

The Goldman Sachs Foundation granted me the chance of a lifetime: participate in an eleven-week, multiplatform program at Babson College, one of the country's leading entrepreneurial programs—for free! My investment was time and energy. The program is called 10,000 Small Businesses (10KSB). Its mission is to educate 10,000 small business owners to help strengthen the US economy.

Within two weeks of being in the program, a wave of anger washed over me. I realized that as a long-time business owner,

I really didn't understand the fundamentals of running a successful business. I felt I had spun my wheels in trying to learn how to run a business, and the many seminars and programs I'd paid for provided little value for creating a successful business. I struggled through a number of the entrepreneurial classes.

Of course, I assumed that I was the only one, but I wasn't. Even folks with master's degrees had difficulty with some of the lessons. But each session was practical and based on research, facts, and proven business-ownership processes. Sessions began with the foundation of each step, the information most of us were never taught. I especially struggled with the finance section.

Some classes required that we tap into our own stories of why we ran our businesses the way we did. I had a light-bulb moment when I suddenly realized why I worked so hard for my business to succeed: I did not want a devastating failure that would traumatize my family. I'd honestly never pulled it all together until that moment. And, yes, I was the first student to cry in class. In adult school. It was a vulnerable time for many of us as we examined why we were in business and then took steps to revive that initial passion. Only this time, we were relaunching our businesses using new, more efficient tools.

All of the instructors were, or had been, successful entrepreneurs and business owners. They were kind and reminded us often that we have to figure out what's needed at each step of developing and expanding our businesses. They emphasized that we don't need to master every task pertaining to our businesses. But we must understand why it's necessary, who can do the job accurately, and what next steps it produces. Most important, we need to know what questions to ask.

Once I understood what I didn't know to ask, the program changed the way I communicated with my CPA, my lawyer, and my human resources firm. It was the most methodical way I'd ever thought about my business. And it sure did beat the dive-in-and-see-what-happens method!

Hard Knocks University,
School of Life, or
whatever you *wish* to call
it, *non-formal education*
isn't easy. It's *hit or miss*,
and *you don't know*
what *you don't know*,
so there's
nothing to research.

The curriculum was inspiring and offered tools we could use to take our next steps. It was hard. It required me to focus on the details of my business in a way I'd never done before.

The program took me out of my business for a minimum of ten hours per week via a virtual classroom and homework. Then there were two full weeks on site and in person near Boston. (I'd never seen fourteen inches of snow before.) This was the first time I'd been in school since I studied to be a graphic designer over thirty years ago.

The program was an absolute fire hose of deep and rapid knowledge. It was, to-date, the best strategic action I'd taken for my business. One of the most valuable lessons I learned was that I need to continually step out of my comfort zone to grow personally and to grow my business. And I still need to do that every day. Every. Single. Day.

Three years after the program, I attended Babson's Surge and Grow program to help transition from founder to CEO. The sessions were packed with practical strategies and tactics for a company's exponential growth. It was there that I learned that most businesses hit a major inflection point right before their next growth phase, typically at the first million-dollar year, then before the five-million mark, then eight million, and finally about twenty million. A founder has to create new products and strategies at each inflection point to break through to the next level. All businesses are facing major changes within our industries due to changes in purchasing behaviors as well as automation. One thing I now know for sure: there is no cruise control in business ownership. Innovation, market awareness, workforce development, and strong processes need to be constant focuses.

Investing in Your Business

If, like me, you launched yourself into business ownership without the necessary foundational knowledge, I highly recommend you invest in some good, targeted business-ownership education. It will save you many, many years (and tens of thousands of dollars) of learning business basics the hard way.

I've continued to learn hard lessons since I returned from Babson. I've tolerated less of what was unnecessary and made bigger, riskier decisions. Not all of them paid off immediately. But oh, that lesson journey is sweet when I celebrate a challenging, long-awaited success.

No matter the size of your business—whether you are just starting out, have your first employee, or have just hired your twentieth—seek to learn all you can about the finances, operations, and processes of each area of your business. Do so from a reputable college or program with a focus on entrepreneurship and business ownership. Confirm that instructors who have had successful businesses and grew their teams teach the courses. Do your due diligence. You will, of course, learn from everything everywhere, so be clear on what and how you want to learn. Whatever you do, find ways to keep investing in your business ownership and personal growth knowledge.

Very few of the business owners I speak with ever get accustomed to the ongoing jolts and whiplash of the business roller-coaster ride. But the majority of them say they wouldn't give it up either. They have faith and the knowledge that each wild ride will eventually stop at a place of accomplishment that non-business owners might find hard to understand.

Nothing beats the joy of team effort and that moment of "we did it!" celebration. Or sometimes it's a celebration of the fact that we've survived and not lost everything out of our pockets during the rough ride.

Continuing Education

When we stop seeking new information—about our industries, technology, topics of personal interest, or ourselves—the world begins to leave us behind. Not having knowledge on a topic creates fear. When we don't understand a topic, it's easy to make judgments or assumptions that aren't accurate. Or we take on inefficient business processes.

I love reading the stories of other business owners and entrepreneurs. And listening to interviews of great leaders can add knowledge to an old process or way of thinking, which often leads to creative solutions to business problems.

Innovation is powered by research and the exploration of new combinations. Entrepreneurial trend-and-pattern spotters are constantly introducing different ideas and methods.

There's so much great information available that we can apply to our work processes. As business owners, we must continually seek out and tap into this knowledge. Reach for a piece of wisdom via an inspiring podcast, book, or business biography. Fill your head with innovative ideas on how to better run your business. Apply them, tweak them, and make them your own.

You'll find a list of my favorite inspirational business resources on my website at FabiPreslar.com. Reinventing what already exists through our own trial and error is not a smart way to work.

Full Circle: Framing Your Story

What resources have you invested in to lead a profitable, successful business?

What's missing from your personal knowledge that can help you propel your business?

What tools do you use to tap into the knowledge of other leaders and business owners you admire?

Innovation is powered
by *research* and
the *exploration* of
new *combinations*.
Entrepreneurial
trend-and-pattern
spotters are *constantly*
introducing different
ideas and methods.

Fear, when not properly managed, is at best a time waster, at worst a recipe for business failure, and somewhere in the middle a barrier to positive energy flowing in your business. Identify your fears and make a plan to overcome them.

CHAPTER 5

Fear

The Fungus among Us

One of the nastiest *F* words I know is fear. It destroys love, reason, decency, creativity, compassion, logic, sanity, and forward motion. It's taken over our planet like a big, invisible fungus, spreading into every community, every business, and every human mind.

I'm not speaking of the rational fear of survival from a violent enemy or the panic we feel when a snake or a bear crosses our path. I'm talking about the fear generated by our overprotective egos (see chapter 3)—the one that tries to warn us of dangers that aren't really dangerous, such as speaking in front of a crowd or raising our rates to get paid more profitably. That same fear repels goodness and suppresses our immune systems. That fear—the fungus among us—is the one in our stories about ourselves, the stories birthed through ignorance, misinterpretation, and procrastination. I know this because I grew up consumed with fear.

Fear Isn't "Pretty"

Despite my French and Italian heritage, I grew up as a Southern gal who wouldn't dream of showing fear. No, no, no, darling, fear isn't pretty—it must be concealed. It's much more proper to talk about anxiety and stress. I mean, my goodness, I'm a business owner; stress is to be expected.

I hid behind the word "stress" for a long, long time. Then I heard Tony Robbins say that stress was simply "fear in disguise," which made me shift my story. I became even more clever at hiding my fear from myself.

Here's how deep it runs: I was into this book's third draft before I realized I'd left out the chapter on fear. The page titled "Fear" actually remained blank. Blank! You know, "because I wasn't really sure what I was going to write about it," said my twisty, two-year-old self wearing a frilly dress and wringing her hands.

You see, that's how absolutely tricky fear can bc.

There's avoiding fear, fighting fear, and facing fear. I sometimes have the illusion I'm doing all of the above, but the truth is, fear can't be fought. It's like a flame that burns brighter when it's fanned with avoidance, antianxiety medication, and denial. It will have to be dealt with—faced rationally—at some point.

We all experience tragedy, failure, rejection, and trauma at some point in our lives. It takes deep courage to look fear straight in the eye during these difficult times. Don't get me wrong—there will be serious times when you can't deal with it head-on during the trauma. It's OK to have a bridge to help you through the really tough times, but make it a temporary bridge. Be true to your feelings and the situation at the time. Take time to heal and grieve when necessary. Be clear that not every fear-filled event will require this bridge. Each of us has our own way of grieving and healing. Yet in the end, facing our fears makes life more authentic and more loving.

I should note that clinical depression and fear are related but not the same thing. Depression frequently requires professional guidance and expertise to help take the best next steps for you. Don't delay or think it will just go away.

Fear Revealed

I'm getting a little wiser about my relationship with my fear. After a great deal of personal-development reading, I've made an agreement with my body that if I'm ignoring or hiding fear, my body will reveal it to me. (Authors like Wayne Dyer, Louise Hay, Anita Moorjani, Mike Dooley, and Brené Brown are among my favorites.) My body has taken on this task with great pride and enthusiasm.

If I'm being rigid and controlling: backache. If I'm avoiding obstacles, hiding from fear, or wishing things were different: migraine. If I'm unhappy with a situation yet avoid making the needed adjustments and blame others instead: anxiety. If I'm taking on other folks' issues and not setting healthy boundaries: neck and shoulder pain. All of these symptoms ultimately pile up, creating more stress within my body and emotions as they inevitably break down my immune system.

Once, a bunch of future-focused issues brought up fear, so I decided to put those concerns on the back burner of life. My body alert came in the form of a weird under-skin fungus that popped up on my back. Gross as those red splotches were, they provided great inspiration for the subtitle of this chapter.

And then there's fear-induced anxiety. I've learned to speak in public and now actually enjoy it. But one day, one of my mentors, Matt, sent me an email stating, "Be ready to share your cold sales call presentation tomorrow. We're going to role-play." All of a sudden my chest and throat turned into hot, prickly concrete. Seriously, I could barely breathe. As soon as I made sure I wasn't having a heart attack, I began asking myself some big questions. For example, now that I'd learned how to speak in public, why was an audience of one giving me a volatile reaction?

I'd intensely avoided my fear of a cold sales call. Can you really fear sales? No. I feared the callous rejections. I feared facing a process that I loathed. My body was making me painfully aware that I feared and detested the process of learning the steps involved in cold calling for business development. My throat and chest hurt for hours afterward. Yes, fear can really freak out your body.

My body has become my warning light for all my fear-hiding mental trickery—as well as revealing that cold calls are just not my style of doing business. Are you so fortunate to have this alert system? A painful crick in the neck or a slipped disc or another physical symptom that we think will hurt less than facing the truth is a powerful cue to examine our fears.

How do you make such an agreement with your body? It may be through an intentional request to your inner wisdom. For some, it's a prayer. The key is to get silent, get clear, and ask for internal help. It's amazing how your body will respond. It's most likely already manifesting your fear, so maybe your "request" could be to be aware or to better interpret the "message" your body is sending.

I've often had to ask myself: How do I hide fear? How does fear rule me? Why am I not moving forward? Here are some of the ways fear might manifest.

Excuses: *I can't because I don't know how. I'm not smart enough to figure it out. I'll get rejected.*

Doubts: *Who do I think I am? I'm too young. I'm too old. I don't have the credentials, the looks, the talent, the money …*

Hesitation: *If I take this leap, I may fail. I'll just wait and see what happens next. What would my family think if I broke tradition?*

Hiding: *If I sink down low and hide, they'll never know I can't do it. I'm too tired to even think about making changes. What's the use?*

Laziness and procrastination: *It might hurt to exercise. It will hurt to start exercising. It's too hard to do business development. Maybe later I'll be ready. I really don't want to feel the pain of change.*

These other manifestations may or may not be issues for you. Still, it may be revealing to ask yourself these fear-busting questions:

- What are my moon-shot business goals? Why haven't they happened?
- Why am I not in peak physical condition?
- Did I take four consecutive weeks of vacation time in the past year?
- Why isn't my annual salary my monthly salary?
- What task have I been avoiding for no good reason?

Did these questions bring you a tinge of anger? Did you suddenly start tuning out? Did you immediately have an excuse? That's your mind using a manifestation of fear to shield you from something it perceives as potentially dangerous. The mind is so very powerful.

Here's the great news: facing your fears, taming your mental demons, and stepping out with a healthy level of ego is seriously empowering. Not only does it begin to change the energy of your business and make it more magnetic and attractive, but also it is an amazing process to not be tethered by fear. Sure, it will pop up and constantly test us, but we now know the conversations to have with ourselves and our guides; we get better at finding the most profound questions to ask of ourselves and of others to take us to our next step. Sometimes that next step is our next phase, and often it is simply to get us to our next day. Learning to talk through fear will be the best gift you can ever give your business. As powerfully draining as fear can be on our businesses and ourselves, releasing fear and its constant play for power is seriously empowering, and it will leave you feeling rather fabulous!

False Evidence Appearing Real

There's no better creative exercise than finding evidence of how and why your fear is real. Think about that for a while.

There is, of course, a healthy level of fear that keeps us from taking undue risks or gambling with an opportunity that could seriously damage our businesses or our health. Perhaps in those cases, it isn't fear at all but well-earned knowledge or perhaps intuition.

Take time to discover what triggers fear within you. Is it from situations or behaviors from your past? Is that still valid today with all you know and the resources you have?

The time spent trying to prove that your fear is rational or justified is quite possibly wasted time. Fear will halt your forward movement. It's up to each one of us to face our fears and identify what we truly want to accomplish.

Full Circle: Framing Your Story

How is fear holding your health and/or business hostage?

List the top five ways fear is showing up and slowing down your business growth.

What clue is your body revealing to you about the state of your thoughts or business?

The *time* spent
trying *to prove* that
your *fear* is rational
or *justified*
is quite possibly
wasted time.
Fear will halt your
forward movement.

Learn to recognize when and how you create fog as a coping mechanism. Then tell yourself a new story that leads you back to the sunshine.

CHAPTER 6

Feeling It Roll In

I wasn't a good salesperson. I made every transaction personal, and every rejection felt like a dagger to the heart.

My company needed me to step into the sales role. Colleagues and mentors tried to convince me that sales is just a numbers game. But when I decided it was time for me to develop new business leads and make the necessary phone calls, I just didn't. It's not that I couldn't; I just didn't, which created an inner turmoil that I chose to ignore.

The next thing I knew, a fog began rolling into my mind. It hid important details and kept me from seeing and attracting opportunities. I couldn't deal with complexity. I became strictly reactive, handling urgent requests and putting out brush fires, but not doing the work needed to move my business forward. In my fog, I resorted to procrastination and daydreaming, usually brought on by some sort of overwhelming situation.

I'm typically empowered by situations that require my talents or a creative solution but not when fog gets in the way. Everything feels too complex.

Procrastination (avoidance) is a good indicator that we, as

business owners, have become foggy-headed. We may make any excuse to avoid the task of creating a complex invoice or tackling year-end tax prep. It's easy to find other things to occupy our time and keep us from having to face whatever it is we don't want to do.

This kind of overwhelmed feeling is often a product of fear. If we're not facing the obstacles ahead of us, chances are it's because we're afraid to take steps to get needed resources or afraid to be rejected or afraid to fail.

And the fog settles in thicker.

Seeing the Fog

If I'm questioning whether I'm in a fog, all I have to do is look around at my current surroundings. I check out the surfaces in my home, car, and office. Has my dining room table become a holding zone for everything coming into my house? Are there stacks of paper in front of the keyboard on my office desk because every single thing is super important?

The spaces where we live and work reflect our emotional states. We stop seeing the things around us when they begin to be too much to deal with. If I discover clutter and chaos that I hadn't really noticed until now, then it's likely there's some heavy fog in my head.

I'm not describing "creative clutter," which indicates I'm in the midst of doing exciting things, but those piles of crappy things I really don't want to do. These to-dos don't just build up physically; they muddle my state of mind.

It's a survival mechanism of sorts. A foggy brain helps us filter out our current realities. If we can't deal with it, we will just stop seeing it. Wow. Isn't the brain brilliant?

I sometimes try to disguise my own fog: "I'm fine, just a bit stressed out," I say. "Oh, this mess? It's part of my creative process."

Unfortunately, fear and fog *are* typically part of my creative process. And people tend to assume that being stressed out is just part of the deal when you're a business owner. But it doesn't have to be that way.

The very opposite of that is a sterile desk with no signs of activity. I suspect that could be another way of hiding in a fog. I really can't speak to that. The chances of me having a sterile desk are extremely unlikely.

Let's stay aware of the fog warnings.

Purge from Within

We can begin by clearing those countertops and desks and even going on to cleaning drawers and closets, but it's time to purge some internal fog and clutter too. As we do our mundane decluttering, we must allow our deepest questions to surface.

Perhaps the overwhelmed feeling is a result of losing track of ultimate goals or the goal paths we set. I don't know about you, but I'm especially good at making a decision, calling it a goal, and then failing to assign the action steps needed to achieve it. Fog can also creep in if we've created an unproductive detour off our goal paths. Lifting the fog requires a search for the questions that will help clarify exactly where we are aiming to end up. What do we really want to accomplish?

It's like getting in the car without a destination. Do you have a map? How about an address to plug into the GPS? If not, how will you know if you're on or off the path? Without a destination, you have no idea where you may end up. And it's never fun driving through fog, especially without direction as to where you intended to go.

Wake Up!

I see many people within their own fog, sleep-walking through life. I recognize their fog because I've learned to see my own. And I know that it's tempting to settle under a cozy blanket of foggy illusion.

For some, it involves procrastination, depression, overeating, undereating, or self-medicating with alcohol or sleep aides. Many of us are guilty of spending too many hours of the day in a heavy fog while staring at the computer, aimlessly lurking on social media, or getting sucked into any of the millions of rabbit holes on the Internet. Meanwhile our to-do lists grow. Nothing gets checked off, and the overwhelmed feeling takes over. As awful as it feels, we often fail to see the problem when we're lost in the fog.

Many small business owners go to networking events with smiles and blank stares. Hands are shaken, cards exchanged, and the words *"couldn't be better"* and *"business is awesome"* ring throughout the room.

When I am fog-free and clear-headed, I'm able to see some of these business owners with clear eyes. And with great empathy. Many look like tired zombies trying to convince themselves they are really OK.

It's tough out there, folks. Business is not always easy, but it doesn't have to wipe us out and throw us into a fog. We need to stay awake to our own realities. The first step is knowing the fog exists and how to break through it. It's about constantly checking in with ourselves and making self-care a top priority.

There are way too many challenges on our planet and too much work to be done in our communities and businesses for us to dwell in the fog. Wake up! No one else can live your life for you, and it takes clear-headed vision to grow your business. Ask yourself the right questions and be ready to answer them from deep within. And if you can't find the right questions, find someone who can help you in your search.

Often the fog sets in when our own stories are no longer working for us. That's OK. Change the plot. In fact, jump up and shout, "Plot change!" Rewrite your own story. And stop beating yourself up. When we change our stories, we change our beliefs about who we are and what we can do.

Take my story, for instance. Continuing to repeat that I suck at sales and will never be a salesperson is a broken record of fear-based beliefs and bad information. My new story is that I know the value that my business and services bring to clients who need them. I don't need to sell. However, I do need prospective clients to be aware that my business is available to them, I'm here to help them, and my services can positively impact their business. And I am really, really good at bringing this opportunity to them. That's a fog lifter right there.

You too can create a new and improved story, so you don't need to hide in foggy fear.

Full Circle: Framing Your Story

What in your business
is too challenging for
you to face head-on?

What shows up in your life to
let you know you're in a fog
or that the fog is rolling in?

What new story will
you create about how
you powerfully lead
your business?

Fear, indecision, facing bad decisions, and second-guessing yourself can lead to a deep freeze where nothing gets done. Your guides and peers can help you thaw out.

CHAPTER 7

Frozen

A Progressive Freeze

Fear can freeze you in your tracks.

I reasoned that because I am a make-things-happen kind of person, this would never happen to me. Everything I'd achieved in business was the result of action. I'd pushed through, gathered a team, jumped over obstacles, and done whatever it took to move forward. So it made no sense that in the midst of one of my biggest business challenges, I froze, just froze. I disguised it, but I froze.

I had made what seemed, on profitability reports, to be a good decision. I stopped promoting and accepting new jobs in our custom-book publishing division.

All the reports showed that these book projects were barely break-even. It was a hard decision to make because this was the only division in which I had maintained an active role in production. And I absolutely loved it. I loved conducting the one-on-one strategy sessions and the creative brainstorming meetings. I loved taking a business owner's vision and goals and creating a professionally packaged product that would provide them with an effective tool to build and fuel their platform.

Over the years, I've excelled in my ability to tune in to the clients who join me for one-on-one strategy sessions. Depending on the client and where they are in life, some sessions are straightforward and informative. But most sessions involve conversations that reveal cleverly hidden issues as to what's keeping them from writing or from discovering their focus or audience. Most of these sessions have brought great insights for both the client and me. I've developed some cool listening and questioning skills within these conversations.

No Profit, No Project

But various business courses made it clear—if it isn't profitable, cut your losses and let it go.

At the time, our custom-book publishing division was the smallest part of our business, and I made the decision to let it go without even consulting my CPA. But I'd missed something important, and unfortunately, I didn't realize it until it was too late to turn things around for that year. In addition to bringing me joy, the custom books served another vital role: spring cash flow.

The spring of each year has notoriously been our slow time. And that's when the majority of books and their initial payments came in. Data and reports would have clearly told me that financial story, if I'd thought to look at them, but I didn't.

That was the first mistake in a series of bad decisions.

The next was a mishandled opportunity (in other words, a mistake). I'd decided I really needed a salesperson, but instead of hiring one, I hired an amazingly wonderful assistant whom a recruiter had found. I'd never had a full-time assistant and didn't know how to properly utilize her skills. Months later, after she'd proven herself, I empowered her as our office manager. She kept the office humming, organized, and fairly joyful.

During that time, we had several clients who became increasingly difficult to manage. We also had a transition within

Ultimately, it is
your decision,
but getting
multiple *perspectives* and
hearing the *experiences
of others* can help
you *make* a more *informed
business decision.*

our team that ended dramatically. And the new designer I'd hired was delightful but couldn't grasp the complexity of the work, so she was transitioned out as well. With cash flow issues, turnover, and challenging clients, I couldn't focus on business development. I didn't realize it at the time, but I not only had gone through some fog but also was gradually shutting down.

Then my assistant began to change. She became less proactive and had fallen back in her role of keeping my to-do list moving forward. I feel sure it was directly due to me not being the easiest person to deal with in my fearful state of being. And I probably felt that she should have been able to read my mind. She couldn't, and no one can.

I slid into a frozen zone; everything felt overwhelming.

It was time to let go of several long-time clients whose negativity was weighing us all down. Their money was important, but they were unfocused, required too much unnecessary attention, and were ungrateful. They were no longer a good fit for our sparkly firm. I raised their prices, and they went away, but not without loads of drama.

I second-guessed myself. How could I have let all that money walk out the door? But I held everything together the best I could, showing a brave face and a smile (sometimes).

Then we lost two large, consistent clients. We felt blindsided. These were long-term contracts that were either sold or sent back out to bid. All work stopped until further notice.

I'd already tapped into my equity line of credit to keep staff on during the cash crunch. And I'd cut Larry's and my salary too. I needed to make the decision to let my beloved assistant go.

I froze solid. I felt like any action I took would damage something else. I'd stare at my computer as time zipped by with nothing being accomplished. My to-do list grew longer and longer.

On top of everything else, we were producing our passion-project magazine for the business community at this time. Many people had made promises to contribute toward the project (content and ads) but didn't ante up when the time came. It would be up to my team and me to make it all happen, and we did.

I hired a salesperson to help us out of this mess, but for a variety of reasons, she just helped us dig a deeper hole to nowhere.

I didn't have the energy or the heart to push this heavy boulder of burden uphill much longer.

Thawing Out

I met with several successful industry colleagues to help me get a better perspective on my situation. Two of them, both men, suggested that I'd done all that I could and that it was probably time to close up shop and "do something else." One told me that with the influence and credibility I'd earned in the community, I could leave small business and become a shining star in corporate.

I sat with that thought, tears in my eyes, as I drove back to the office. That's when I felt the fire come through my core. The first wave of thawing had begun.

I am not done yet! I have so much left to give and to do, and this business will not only survive but also thrive.

I believe that the colleagues with whom I spoke were my gift in this situation, and I harbor no anger about their perspectives. I was frozen and had lost my spark. Telling me that I might have done all I'm capable of doing lit me up. I am actually deeply grateful.

I scheduled time with my guides, who immediately got to work asking me the big questions and creating steps to rebuild my business and myself. I had gotten pretty beat down.

Every business owner I've talked with has felt frozen

through fear at one time or another. It's these situations that often end up fueling our internal fires. And this is when it's critical to have people who understand our journeys (and don't benefit directly from them) to help talk us through the tough spots.

I recommend having several folks play this role with you as each will bring a unique perspective. The partners I pay for business services will have different perspectives than the guide I pay to ask me deep questions or the friends who know my personal journey. When I've made difficult decisions that I know will rock the worlds of staff, clients, vendors, and myself, these are often the decisions my advisors, masterminds, and guides have helped me get to. Ultimately, it is your decision, but getting multiple perspectives and hearing the experiences of others can help you make a more informed business decision.

It's up to each of us to fuel our internal fires to keep the chill of a fear-freeze from coming on. The chance of freezing solid is greater when we don't have realistic outside perspectives and cheerleaders. Having champions and cheerleaders who believe

Having *champions* and *cheerleaders* who *believe* in us during *tough times* is *priceless*. When our *personal* skills are *pushed* to the *edge* of our *knowledge*, we *cannot go it alone.*

in us during tough times is priceless. When our personal skills are pushed to the edge of our knowledge, we cannot go it alone.

Let's become cheerleaders and voices of reason for one another. Business ownership isn't easy. It requires great courage, and it requires a great team of advisors, guides, and friends.

Oh, and when you have conversations with those you trust, stop with all the acting like everything is OK and you're just fine all the time. That serves no one.

Full Circle: Framing Your Story

Who are the business advisors whom you can trust to tell the whole truth?

Who are your five cheeriest cheerleaders who can help you thaw your freeze?

What is your public language about your business like?

When times are challenging, do you at least hint that there's room for help? Or is everything "just fine"?

Sometimes business owners create successful, confident facades but really feel like frauds. Remove the illusion of being an impostor by gaining confidence in yourself and your skills and by managing your expectations of yourself and others.

CHAPTER 8

Facade

The Impostor

As a business owner, have you ever built a facade because you felt like a fraud? Like some kind of impostor? Do the requirements of innovation and growth in the "fake it till you make it" model leave you feeling like a fraud-filled faker?

I have. That feeling of being an impostor comes from believing our worst fears about ourselves. For example, I was once asked to speak on a panel, and I felt that anyone else who was breathing could do a better job than me.

That may have been true, but I quickly realized that I was the one selected, and it would be up to me to rock out the presentation and share whatever knowledge I had. And it turned out that the audience was interested in my know-how after all. They valued my perspective and insights on the topic. Why had I distorted and underestimated what I had to contribute to this group?

Since then, I continue to encounter times when I feel like a fraud. Honestly, it comes with risk-taking and the act of throwing yourself into a situation without knowing everything you think you should know. After years of putting myself in this type of let's-see-what-happens scenario, I've discovered that people with great passion and integrity are the ones who tend to experience this uncomfortable feeling of being an impostor.

Putting yourself in situations in which you've never done what's being asked requires you to create and innovate. And even if others think we already "know it all," we are continually learning.

Woman Business Owner of the Year

An experience that put having a facade and being an impostor into perspective for me was the Woman Business Owner of the Year competition. I was in the midst of still being frozen during my biggest face-punched year in business. I'd taken some big risks that created a perfect storm of disappearing cash, clients, and staff. I needed to let a staff member that my team really, really liked go. And in order to keep the remainder of my team intact, I took out bank loans. Larry and I cut our pay and dipped into our retirement savings, all while working additional hours to make sure our team received their full salaries.

I was still trying to recuperate from this ordeal when I received an email saying, "Congratulations, you've been nominated for Woman Business Owner of the Year."

My computer keyboard put marks on my forehead when I dropped my head onto my desk. I said all sorts of fun *F* words. *What kind of joke was this? What warped person would nominate me and expose such pain?* Naturally, I'd have to decline the nomination.

For three days I worked on typing out an email politely declining this opportunity. It had been seven years since I participated in this competition. I'd actually been a finalist two years in a row. Rather than accomplishments, I saw these experiences as public rejections and failure.

It's *difficult*
to accept
others *celebrating*
you for being
more than
you *believe*
you are.

But then I reconsidered. Even though it was a robust application, my thought was that it'd be easy for me to dig up the old application, update it a bit, and toss it into the competition.

I found the file and read through all the goals I'd set for my business and myself seven years ago. I'd written about how I wanted to grow my team and about the national clients I was building my company to attract.

I couldn't reuse a word of my old application.

Tears trickled down my face as the realization set in: I had accomplished and surpassed every goal I'd set. I'd tripled my business. I had a solid team. I'd been able to hire top talent that included my husband as creative director, a past client as our current communications director, my daughter as production assistant, and two brilliant designers. I'd purchased a building. And we had not only national but also international clients that helped us to be a profitable company year over year.

I took a deep breath and enjoyed a heart-flitter moment of celebration. Then for no other reason than to document what I'd done and what I planned to do with my business, I made the decision to complete the ten-page application. I'd noted who the finalists and winners were for the past few years. All were amazing, inspirational women. I didn't stand a chance anyway, so I had nothing to lose.

I sent an email accepting the nomination and began writing full on, telling the real and raw story of my entrepreneurial journey. Weeks later, word came that the judges had reviewed the applications and named me one of the top three finalists.

All I could do was shout, "Really? You've got to be kidding me!" I felt like the heavens must be playing some kind of joke on me and I'd become someone's personal comedy show. I felt like, yes, a bit of a fraud to be celebrated as a woman business owner of the year during the aftermath of one of my worst years ever.

After a while, I calmed down and decided to create a different story about the situation. My new story went like this: instead of playing tricks on me, God and the heavens knew the storm I was going through and were reminding me that I am deeply supported and that the crisis was temporary, with good things ahead for me and my business. I even went through a scenario that I was about to die and this was a nice way to sum up my life. (Note: not all scenarios are healthy.)

I did all the promotional activity, headshots, bios, and video interviews. And finally, the day came for my in-person interview with the judges. As I left for the interview, my daughter gave me a hug and said, "Mom, you've already won with all that you have done for our family, team, clients, and community." (And there went my carefully applied makeup.)

I had no idea who the judges would be. When I walked into the interview room, I saw my peers, a panel of six rock star women business owners. I felt a bit lightheaded at first, but then I became calm. I was ready to answer their questions with the hardcore truth. Larry and I were scheduled to leave that afternoon for a nine-day getaway to celebrate our wedding anniversary, so I figured that the sooner I was through with this interrogation (oops, I mean interview), the sooner we could head to the beach.

My answers were heartfelt and direct, and I shared my commitment to my business. I was asked why I wanted to win this competition, and I answered the question honestly. I didn't need this win for myself or for my business. I explained that if I did win, however, I would leverage it for the organization and share my story with other business owners.

I surprised myself with my candor. At that point I felt that I had probably lost the competition, but I'd won another level of passion back for my business. The interview wrapped up, and I headed to the beach to celebrate thirty years of marriage to an incredible man and my partner in life, love, and business.

Larry and I returned from beach bumming the day of the awards gala. We dressed up for the event, and I even wore long black gloves, just because I could and have always wanted to.

To my great surprise, I won the title of 2017 Charlotte Woman Business Owner of the Year from the Charlotte chapter of the National Association of Women Business Owners! In the midst of celebrating this honor with my family and colleagues, I snapped a photo of the award and texted it to my staff. In response, they texted me smiley faces, clapping hands, and confetti-horn emojis. It was an exciting evening.

But when I returned to the office the next morning, it was business as usual. Not one of my employees mentioned the award; there was not the tiniest acknowledgment of this honor the entire day, not one word. It cut quite deeply.

To be recognized by sponsors, the community, and my peers for my efforts but to not receive a positive word or gesture from my employees was beyond hurtful and disappointing. That feeling of being a fraud completely overtook me. What kind of awful business owner was I to not be celebrated by the talented people on my team? It would take a great deal of reflection and accountability to take ownership of this glaring issue in our company culture.

This interaction shined a light on serious issues and traumas that had built up within my team. But at that time, I was frozen in fear and pushed these issues aside, right along with my own pain and my disappointment in the company culture and facade that I'd created.

In hindsight, this moment created a personal breakdown that led to a personal and business breakthrough, but that wouldn't happen for a few more months. My strong facade stayed loosely tacked on.

Breaking Expectations

The feeling of being a fraud or an impostor can come from expectations we have of those around us. It can also come from a strong, underlying fear that we're not good enough.

It's difficult to accept others celebrating you for being

Fear can
easily *take over*
and make us more
sensitive to the
smallest of
perceived failures.

more than you believe you are, especially in the midst of challenging times. These are the times when self-confidence lags and we feel most vulnerable. Fear can easily take over and make us more sensitive to the smallest of perceived failures.

I hear too many stories about business owners having their feelings shattered by employees who blindside them. My team didn't do anything to me, but the experience did expose issues that I needed to examine.

Relationships with my employees have been a challenge for me since day one. I've learned that releasing personal expectations changes everything and makes interactions easier. Our validation as business owners should never be dependent on positive acknowledgment from our team. And if we do receive a kind word along the way, then it's a double kindness.

After winning this cool award, my family of personal cheerleaders stepped up and celebrated the hard work and success with more loving words and affirmation than I could have imagined. I am deeply grateful for their support and for the long way I've been able to come in my life and in my business.

However, facing the hard truths on which a faulty foundation is built requires deep accountability. I took the time and the courage to explore what my role was in creating a culture that didn't feel compelled to mark this honor and that felt no reason to celebrate me. I had made a great many mistakes and difficult decisions and didn't take the care or time to share what was going on with my team. It created a culture of fear and disengagement. They had, after all, expressed their feelings in festive emojis the night of the event.

So feeling like a fraud and impostor in this case was quite valid. I had seriously important work to do, and it was proven to me quite clearly. So I did the humbling work, which included further right-sizing my ego.

Twelve months after this humbling lesson, I was confidently able to commemorate my title as Woman Business Owner of the Year as I gave a quick speech on what this award meant to me. That celebration and speech came as I announced the next very deserving Woman Business Owner of the Year. Fascinatingly enough, several days later the *Charlotte Business Journal* awarded my firm the honor of First-Generation Family Business of the Year. A very different celebration took place the next day. The entire team stood in a huddle and talked about the event and the win. We did so over the cake, balloons, and handmade congratulatory cards that the team had pulled together before work that morning. What an amazing feeling it was to celebrate not only the award but also how far we'd come as a team.

Next time that feeling of hiding behind a facade or being an impostor comes over you, how will you change your internal conversation? Perhaps it's a mirror of the real situation you are in. Or maybe it's driven by internal fear. Either way, I've learned it is worth taking the courage to explore. I encourage you to check the facade and impostor that may be masking your situation.

Full Circle: Framing Your Story

What is your business facade?

What personal expectations
do you have of your team?

As the feeling of being an
impostor comes up, what
questions will you ask yourself?

Turn your failures into fuel. Failure is an opportunity to change, to redirect to something even better, and to fuel your business more than you could ever imagine.

CHAPTER 9

Failure

The Opportunity in Redirection

Failure is not only good fuel but also a good indicator of whether we're headed in the right direction. The need to redirect in the midst of failure can be painful, but I've found that the less I resist, the sooner a new path is revealed.

My business has always reflected my lifelong drive for independence and freedom. Three years into producing and publishing my own local business magazine, I realized that I was thinking and acting way too small with an audience with whom I was way too comfortable. The local business audience was what I knew best, but it kept me from stretching past my comfort zone. Ultimately, this audience exhausted me.

I thought about all the effort and resources I was devoting to this aspect of my business. I'd given this group of business owners all I had, but my own business had gained nothing directly from them. It was painful to look at this situation with such honesty. With counsel from my guides, I realized that a major redirection was necessary.

It was difficult at first to focus on my personal growth and my company's future. But the redirection led me to seek my next audience and to take my business to new heights.

Redirection is often riddled with resistance to new ways, new paths, new people, and new processes. Change is unsettling, but to quote Jessie Potter, director of the National Institute for Human Relationships, during her address at the Seventh Annual Woman to Woman Conference, "If you always do what you've always done, you always get what you've always gotten."

Public Speaking

Years ago, I was invited to pitch my business in *the Make Mine a Million $ Business (M3)* competition, which was like an *American Idol*® for business meets *Shark Tank*® live on stage. I'd previously taken a speaker's boot camp course, so I knew how to share my business story, and I was clear on the value that I was providing my clients. The judges critiqued the delivery of my practice pitch the evening before the competition and gave me feedback that my overall vision wasn't clear enough, that my presentation lacked vision.

Based on that one bullet point from the critique, I revamped my entire presentation. I worked late into the night consolidating about ten data points of additional information into my three-minute pitch. I didn't sleep at all—not a wink. And when I stood on stage in front of 400 people for the competition the next day, I went brain-fogged-tongue-tied-stupid. In hindsight, I wish I'd had the confidence to adjust just that one talking point. Instead, I lost confidence in my entire presentation.

This was a highly promoted event with lots of media attention. I had a wonderful group of supportive girlfriends there to cheer me on, as well as many local business owners. Out of the nineteen finalists who pitched their businesses that day, only three didn't reach the winning status. I was one of the three.

It was painful, and the internal judging machine in my head worked on full blast for many days.

A *business owner* who *fails* is *not a failure.* You failed simply because there was a *better direction, better audience,* or *better* way. *Find out* what that is and then *start again.*

I later turned that failure into fuel by learning how to speak in public without a script. I also learned that there are numerous ways to present information.

Sometimes I can't include all the data, talking points, and information I'd like to convey into the allotted time. What's more important is that I engage the audience, share my enthusiasm, and aim to inform, rather than to win. Aiming to win, for the sake of winning, is a formula for failure, which I'd already learned the hard way. I now focus on being authentic whenever I'm speaking to a group.

I recently had a client call me in a panic. She asked me if I would fill in for a keynote speaker who had been in an accident. I was given a two-hour notice to drive across town and speak at a luncheon.

Although I was wearing blue jeans and not dressed for such an opportunity, I confidently accepted the challenge, knowing I would be helping out my client. It gave me an opportunity to deliver an impromptu keynote without notes at a luncheon with over fifty business executives.

Knowledge, practice, review, and opportunity brought me to that moment. And all of it was fueled by my earlier failure.

Failure Not an Option

"Failure is not an option" was my motto when I first started my business. I was adamant: I could not and would not fail. I believed that failing was a sin of the weak and the ignorant. After all, in my childhood I'd experienced that not knowing how to make a business succeed could cause devastating failure. The pain of that journey created an extreme and false belief about failure.

With a lineage of failed business ownership running through my blood, it's clear why I'd demand such a decree. But I wish everyone who heard me say that would have punched me. Instead, I heard affirmations like, "You go, girl!" or "Amen, sister!"

If I could go back in time, I'd turn that motto on its head: "I must fail ten times before I know I'm on the track to success."

That's madness, I can hear my old self say. *That's just setting yourself up for failure.*

Exactly! Business cannot be its best until we know what its worst is. It cannot grow beyond our expectations if we hold on tightly to our safe, limited expectations.

Failure hurts if we're attached to it.

Failure hurts if we keep reliving it.

OK, plan A failed, so let's move on to plan B with what we've learned. As Norman Lear would succinctly say it, "Over and next."

"I'm a failure." Nope, not unless you decide you are. A business owner who fails is not a failure. You failed simply because there was a better direction, better audience, or better way. Find out what that is and then start again.

Holding on to a project or idea that is failing is the worst thing you can do. These attachments will make you sick. And you can go broke. A failure that is not released will gain momentum and drag you along with it. No good can come of it until you redirect it.

The sooner you accept that your present action is failing, the sooner you can redirect your energies or find a solution to the problem. Even if *you* are the problem. The fact is, I've been the problem in most of my failures.

Once we make the shift in how we process our mistakes, we eventually stop labeling every business decision that doesn't work out as a "failure." We call it trial and error. Or we determine that it was the right idea at the wrong time or the right product but the wrong audience. We eventually learn to understand that these missteps are critical to our success.

Imagine what would happen if our business licenses required that we fail ten times. Might that keep us from settling into safe little businesses that never stretch our talents?

My goodness, what might I have accomplished in the past twenty years if I wasn't afraid to fail? What might *you* accomplish if you aren't afraid to fail?

Failure as Fuel

Failures knock me down for a while. Some can be a real face-punch.

After every speech, every event, every meeting, and every project, I become hyperfocused on the things that went wrong. I analyze every misstep and misspeak. What could have been done better? What was omitted? Why did I feel this way or that way?

It's an exhausting process. Some might call this self-sabotaging behavior, but in truth, I don't see my hindsight reflection as a negative. I see it as an emotional retrospective, a sort of redux introverted analysis.

I can look back at the film-like mental images of past actions and watch myself with more detachment and with less self-judgment.

There was a time when reviewing my perceived missteps and errors resulted in me blaming and punishing myself. But now I've gained a bit of wisdom and use this reflection as a tool for identifying those things I could have done better. I open myself to new insights. And the fact is, any experience we go through gives us the know-how to do it better the next time. There is always room for improvement. Or at some point you decide it is as it needs to be and then focus on other areas.

I now also take time to acknowledge specific things that went well and times that I was rocking awesome. I celebrate these with gratitude.

I review my mistakes, omissions, and blunders not to beat myself up but to make myself better. I can process these failed moments and transform what I've learned into fuel. Fuel to succeed.

Full Circle: Framing Your Story

How do you perceive failure as you grow your business? How has this changed over time?

What personal or professional success was fueled by a past failure?

What do you keep doing even though you don't like the results you keep getting?

What foundational beliefs have you changed from childhood that now strongly impact you and your business?

A *failure that is not released* will *gain momentum* and *drag you along* with it. No good can come of it until you *redirect it.*

Know thyself. You can be true to who you are while also pushing past your comfort zone.

CHAPTER 10

Facets

Be You, Be True, Sparkle On

By necessity, business owners have a variety of different traits we bring to bear in different situations, much like the facets of a gem sparkling in turn when they're in the spotlight. Some of those traits are more comfortable than others—both for us and the people around us.

I'm an introvert and a bit of an empath, and I'm clumsy. At times I'm logical, even to the point of being rigid, while at other times I'm a little woo-woo in my thoughts. There are buttons that launch my wicked temper. (My husband and daughter know exactly where these buttons are, and they're pros at avoiding them or, at times, pushing them with all their might.) If you've disrespected my business or someone in my inner circle, you'll meet my snarky side or my temper. I laugh at my own jokes, while those around me just drop their shaking heads. I love humor, silliness, and sarcasm, as long as they're not intended to hurt someone.

I avoid crowds. And yet I like the stage because I can feel the entire crowd all at once and at a short distance. After I'm around people for any length of time, I need to collapse and sleep for several hours to recharge. My immediate assumption is that folks don't like me, and I'm pretty sure I'm often correct.

If I care about you, I'll be brutally honest and mirror something about yourself back to you that you may wish to deal with. My aim is never to hurt you; instead, it's to awaken something within you. I rarely do this without your permission. However, there have been situations where my truthfulness has caused someone to ban me from their life (which actually has saved us both a great deal of time). But my honesty has also been the catalyst for deep, authentic conversations and soul-satisfying relationships.

The questions I'm compelled to ask during the strategy sessions I conduct with my clients serve my business well. I help entrepreneurs and professionals create highly customized books and magazines to fuel their platforms. My natural talents are put to good use in the service of my clients.

It's taken me many years to become comfortable in my own skin. I think each personal transformation brings on a new level of self-confidence. Or maybe it's emotional scar tissue from each transformation that simply creates a thicker skin. I'm not yet wise enough to know the difference.

There have been folks in my life who can't accept me for who I am and whom I'm striving to become. In most of those cases, I've needed to move on and attract a better inner circle of confidants. It's not an easy thing to do, but it sure makes for a beautiful life of authentic living. All this is to say, know who you are and what you bring to each relationship, event, and meeting. The you that shows up in your life and your business really needs to be the authentic you.

Too "Peopley": The Introverted Entrepreneur

As I've mentioned, I'm an introvert. Many entrepreneurs are. I do believe we need to be keenly aware of who we are and what we bring to our businesses and any social situations.

Know *who you are*
and the level
of *who you are*
that *you bring* to each
relationship, event,
and meeting.
The you that shows
up *in your life* and
your *business*
really *needs* to be
the authentic you.

Introverts and extroverts can both shine brightly; we just each do it differently.

At my first networking events, I'd head straight to the back of the room and try to blend into the wall. I'll never forget the wonderful woman at one of these events who walked up to me and said, "Hey, how are you going to meet anyone if you stand back here by yourself?"

It took a huge amount of practice for me to walk into a crowded room and meet people. But today, I'm the person who helps integrate the newbie introverts in the room. (Maybe it's introvert radar that makes it easier to spot them.) I've made a number of dear friends from this practice. And now, when I get on stage as the keynote speaker, a panelist, or a moderator, people tell me that there's no way I'm an introvert. I graciously accept this reaction as a life-long achievement.

It takes a great deal of energy to be an introvert in public. During conferences where we are packed into learning sessions sandwiched in with people, people, people all day long, you will not see me socializing after hours. I'll be in my room detoxing and recharging for the next day. Within hours after a speech or presentation, I'm curled up asleep or quietly nursing a full-body people hangover. I don't like that this happens, but there seems to be no way to avoid it. If I challenge myself to attend two events in a day, I can delay the effect, but it's foolish to plan anything that requires brain capacity afterward. I'll be incapable of making decisions. Without much-needed recovery time, my speech may become slurred, I may feel like I have the flu, or I may get smacked with a migraine. The key is to manage my energy.

For me, the secret to networking is to assign myself a purpose or task at each event. In the early years of business ownership, I often contacted the organizer or host prior to the event to see how I might be of service that day. Jobs may have included placing fliers in the seats or checking in guests and handing them their nametags. Most often the greeters at these events are introverts because we introverts understand how helpful it is to have a purpose and an introduction.

What also works well for me is sponsoring a spotlight or expo table at the event to introduce my company. I'm able to talk about my business with no problem.

My main task, if I'm not a speaker at the event, is to walk into the room and stop to say hello to at least five people individually. Most folks at networking events are there to grow their networks and are open to meeting others. However, I've also been to cliquey events where small groups boxed me out of conversations. I didn't attend those again.

As an introvert, I've got to be "in the groove" to meet and be surrounded by people. I've been known to walk into an event and stay for a minute or two, feel that I'm just not into it, and walk back out to go home. Or if I've had a tight schedule, and these events feel too "peopley" to handle with my current energy level, I'll cancel several of them for a number of consecutive days. I've spent a fair amount of money on events I didn't attend, but I've spent far more on events that I did attend. I never cancel an event if I have a role or if I'm a speaker. When I have a clear purpose for being there, I find the energy I need.

Over the years I've pushed the boundaries of my introversion to the max, transforming myself into somewhat of a functional ambivert. I can flip when required to do so, but it's essential that I manage my energy afterward. I insist on silence whenever possible and cannot tolerate ongoing noise around me. It drives my staff crazy to have such a quiet work environment, but that's why they make personal headsets. Right?

Love in Business

I've taken many personality assessments over the years, and many of them identify "love" as my deepest value.

I'm not surprised. For me, everything eventually comes down to love. It is the goal, the journey, and the endgame. There are very few problems love can't solve. And whether it's in the form of respect, kindness, or compassion, I strive to reflect love daily. Love is my core; it's my super-soft squishy middle.

It's the cornerstone of my business too, but admittedly, I've made many mistakes as I've tried to bring love into the workplace. I didn't know how to do it properly. Part of the difficulty I've experienced with coworkers, clients, and employees came from me wanting to communicate with them as friends. Unfortunately, wanting to focus on love resulted in me being treated as a pushover. Leading with love takes a strong level of personal discipline and respect for ourselves, as well as respect for others.

It can be difficult to incorporate love at the core of every business transaction without being taken advantage of. I've become more skilled at this through the years. But because people are people, and they all come to us with their own bag of issues, I still get blindsided at times. There are many who just don't play fair or are so focused on sales and profit that compassion and love for team and clients is nonexistent.

Regrettably, I have a quick temper. What happens when it's triggered doesn't sound or look like love. Often my anger is a form of self-protection. Sometimes it's directed at the lack of honesty or kindness within the present business encounter. After an outburst, I have to deal with my own guilt, find forgiveness, and then return to love.

Having a loving, heart-centered business does not mean sacrificing a good profit. In fact, if a business is not profitable, it more than likely means it hasn't been infused with enough love to build strong processes. Love creates the kind of company that generates clients willing to pay for the value your business brings them.

If a *business is not profitable,*
it more than likely means
it *hasn't been infused*
with *enough love* to
build *strong* processes.
Love creates
the kind of *company* that
generates *clients* willing
to *pay for the value*
your *business brings* them.

Accountability

I've always chosen to drive my own life. I didn't always have a roadmap, but I kept my foot on the accelerator and the wheels aimed forward.

It wasn't until I turned thirty that I began to understand that everything that happened to me came from decisions and choices I'd made. Prior to that, despite my independence, I believed that people were doing things to me and creating outcomes for me that I didn't want. I didn't like feeling powerless, but it *was* convenient that I didn't have to take responsibility for anything that wasn't going well in my life.

My early thirties was a time of personal awakening. I learned to become accountable for my thoughts and actions. But the idea of not blaming others took some getting used to. I mean, think of all those folks who held me back and made life more difficult for me. Releasing them from these perceived wrongdoings required a great deal of internal work. And seeing my part in the big picture was humbling.

It was my mentor and guide, Yvonne, who burst my illusion. She'd become fed up with my stories about how folks in business were doing me wrong. It was time for me to grow up and see my role in every single one of those interactions. She was tough yet patient with me on these lessons on accountability.

Here is the truest thing I know about being a business owner: I alone am responsible for the health of my business. Full accountability means accepting that what happens in my business is based 100 percent upon my choices, my frame of mind, and how I build my team.

It's easier to maintain this level of awareness when I'm in a positive state of mind. When I'm in fear mode, it's much harder. During these difficult times, accountability weighs as a burden.

But once I refocus on my desire to creatively attract and serve great clients, the results are fulfilling. Life flows smoothly, and I'm able to see the small miracles happening around me.

Building a New Personal Foundation

Ongoing personal development involves exploring our deep-seated beliefs. These may be beliefs about our histories, our futures, or ourselves. It is powerful, brain-tingling, ego-shattering work.

Early in my relationship with my husband, Larry, he was on a trip and missed calling in at two checkpoints. I panicked and pleaded with God for his safety and to please give me at least thirty great, long years with him. Ultimately, I "made a contract" with my soul for those thirty years. Back then, I was young and that much time seemed like forever. My prayers were answered: Larry returned home safely. Then, as we humans tend to do, I "forgot" about the contract.

As our thirtieth wedding anniversary drew near, the contract date came "due." I may not have remembered the deal I'd made on a conscious level, but my subconscious mind surely did. The knowledge manifested as fear. My body and psyche responded with nightmares and anxiety that Larry's life would soon end. The fear challenged many of my thoughts. I was afraid that if I spoke about it, this dreaded scenario would come true. Fear can apparently block rational logic.

Once I recognized the source of my fear and "remembered" when my contract was made, I also understood that this contract had formed the foundation for many of my personal and business decisions over the past thirty years. In hindsight, my hidden belief of having a timeline may have played a part in us enjoying such a strong relationship.

The question that changed everything for me in this situation was, "You wrote the contract. Why can't you rewrite it?" So, in meditation, I "rewrote" the contract; I made a new deal without any time limit attached. The anxiety and fear that had gripped me were immediately gone.

I began asking myself what other contracts and beliefs were embedded in my personal foundation, impacting my life in ways I wasn't aware of. I'm currently in the process of discovering them. Once I've examined them, I can choose to keep the ones that are valuable and useful and rewrite those that have served their purpose. (This is a fascinating exercise, and I recommend giving it some dedicated thought.)

For most of my life, I've believed that I need to work harder and harder—at times, to the point of exhaustion—to prove my worth. Over the past few years, my dear friend Carla has been pointing this belief out to me. She asks, "When do you think you'll have proven yourself to be enough and stop working so hard?"

Just writing that question brings tears to my eyes. This is a sure indication I need to excavate some blocks from that part of my foundation.

It's one thing to say that our thoughts become things, that we create our own realities, and that to change our circumstances, we must change our attitudes; it's quite another to actively demonstrate these principles in our own lives. I've been able to use these tools to answer some of the "whys" and "hows" in my life and create a better reality. I now know that there's an inner wisdom that is constant, but it's a quiet presence. It's heard when the time is right.

As we work to simplify our lives, silence worthless thoughts, add love, deepen faith, remove paralyzing fear, and rebuild

Leading with love takes a *strong* level of *personal* discipline and *respect* for ourselves, as well as *respect for others*.

personal foundations, we are taking steps to strengthen our force within. May the process beautifully shape our own facets and allow love to create new building blocks for our businesses and ourselves.

Full Circle: Framing Your Story

What authentic talents and personality traits do you bring to your business?

Where is your internal comfort zone? How would your business better thrive if you pushed beyond that comfort?

What internal contracts and foundational beliefs drive your decisions, and how do they affect your business?

What internal contracts do you need to rewrite?

Believe in something both within and outside of yourself. Believe in your ability to create the awesome reality you want. Faith (not necessarily in a religious sense) is needed to have a business that is both heart-centered and profitable.

CHAPTER 11

Faith

Hello, Anyone up There?

By the time I was twenty-nine years old, I'd moved over fifteen times; lost my childhood home; lived with another family; moved alone to a new city with no friends, family, security net, or support; worked my way through college; been hit by a drunk driver and had my car totaled; met and married Larry; given birth to our daughter; and launched and lost my first business.

I learned how to survive and thrive through chaos. I became good at it. When I turned thirty, it seemed that my life had finally calmed down. In fact, it was nearly perfect.

But without warning, a weird emotional reality warp took over. I didn't know how to live without struggle and chaos, without blazing forward in survival mode. I didn't know how not to be totally consumed by work.

Unfortunately, I came to the conclusion that I had lived a very reactive life overpowered by events—my entire life had just "happened" to me, and it was time I got the things I wanted. I felt angry and rebellious. This was probably similar to the phase that most teenagers go through, but I didn't have the luxury of doing so as a young adult. I was too busy surviving.

Every aspect of my life was impacted. I'd become a selfish, hurtful person and had disregarded and disrespected my family. My ego had done its job of protecting me but had become out of control. I was disliked by everyone who loved me. I'd never experienced such anger reflected back at me, and justly so.

Greater than Me

It took a number of months before I began to recognize that this negative life wasn't serving me. I'd pushed away everyone I loved. One day, the full realization of the awfulness I'd created finally crashed down on me. I was overwhelmed with intense sorrow and frustration, and all I knew to do was go outside for a long walk. I needed to find some air and steady my breathing.

My thoughts were wild and rambling as the fresh air filled my lungs. I sensed that I was hitting an emotional rock bottom. And then I went physically and emotionally numb. It was as though I was walking in a heavy cloud, but I began feeling so light my feet didn't seem to touch the ground. (Disclaimer: I've never used drugs, so these experiences weren't chemically induced. My editors felt it best that I include this note.) I couldn't hear my heartbeat. Was I being beamed-up? Had I died? The fear that no one would know, or care, filled my thoughts.

But then an invisible wave of energy ran through me and returned me to my present reality. It was a force both within me and outside of me. It emotionally and spiritually lifted me up and assured me that there was a great deal I needed to learn and a great deal I needed to do. It filled me with humility and the courage to turn around and walk back home. I knew I needed to stop trying to be right and focus instead on being real and vulnerable. I was ready to face the reality of and accountability for everything I'd done wrong and to work on rebuilding my relationships. It was time for me to grow up on an entirely new level.

At that moment, I crossed a spiritual threshold. It marked the start of my journey to figuring out my life—a life that didn't need to be filled with busyness and chaos, a life that was much more than about me and my feelings.

And it was in this moment that I began to accept and truly build my faith.

There have been several incidents in my life in which I've felt the presence of something greater than me and sensed there was something greater that I needed to accomplish. At those times, I felt a deep, loving support that went far beyond the amazing human love I'm surrounded by each day. For me, there's no need for these experiences to be proven or disproven by science or religion. They have helped me grow my faith. And they remind me that what happens in my life is significant and insignificant at the same time.

Faith-Filled Business

My definition of faith is a belief in something that cannot be seen and for which there is no apparent proof. It's a trust in my inner wisdom and a trust in the greater power outside of me. I've had profound spiritual experiences that have convinced me there's something greater than any of us, something unseen that is supporting us and conspiring toward our success.

My business has been a critical part of my spiritual journey. It takes faith beyond knowledge to launch a business from a need or an idea. It takes faith to hire that first employee and give them what feels like part of your income and all of your trust. It takes faith to let go of clients who are no longer a fit and to know your business will be more than OK afterward.

Infusing spirituality in business means keeping the focus on doing for others. It is honoring something greater than profit.

It is bringing genuine value to clients and generating a fair monetary exchange.

Having faith in business is asking a question into thin air and knowing that an answer will come back to you in some form or another. Maybe that question is about a social media campaign, a financial challenge, or how to better respond to a troubled employee. No question is too big or too small.

At my firm, whenever we send out a big proposal or enter client work into a competition, our team gathers together. We wave our "magic SPARKle fingers" toward the project, sending collective intentions for a good outcome. I've never given my staff any instructions, and they came up with the SPARKle fingers. Everyone is free to launch their own level of faith along with the submission. Even if someone didn't work on the proposal or project directly, they still participate in wishing it success.

I can't say for sure it's because of our SPARKly ceremony, but we've won quite a few of those proposals and awards over the years! (A huge part of faith is believing, right?)

Life Swirls

All of us experience situations that bring our lives to a halt and test our faith. Often, it's a series of challenges that surround us and create what I call a "life swirl."

One of my life swirls began with the death of my dear, sweet mother-in-law. Shortly after that, my mentor became terminally ill, and my best friend was diagnosed with epilepsy. All of this happened in the middle of growth strategy issues within my business. I was in the process of transitioning out my entire team and starting over.

I found myself sitting alone in my 1,500-square-foot office in a sad fog. In times like these, I tunnel into a cocoon and concentrate on that timeframe's version of survival. I've learned that picturing myself wrapped up tight in that blue

It takes *faith to hire*
that first *employee*
and *give* them what
feels like part of
your income and
all of *your trust.*
It takes *faith*
to *let go* of clients
who are
no longer a fit.

cocoon allows me to eventually release the wrap of pain a tiny bit to let a crack of light come through. That light comes as some sort of a gifted message sent from "out of the blue." It may pop in via a book or an email, in the words of a compassionate person, or as a unique opportunity that suddenly presents itself.

In this case, it was a phone call with an invitation to speak on creativity in the workplace. I accepted the invitation to be part of a speakers' panel, and there I found myself sitting next to Suzanne, the woman who would introduce me to the Innovation Institute.

Participating in the institute's program helped me to burst out of my own way and reignited my creative core. No, it didn't change any of the painful things around me—in their own time, circumstances transitioned in the ways they needed to—yet this renewed creativity was the gift I needed to launch my next transformation.

Another life swirl happened within the first year of bringing my husband, Larry, on board in my company full-time. That move involved us both taking pay cuts, and we said good-bye to his corporate salary and corporate insurance. At that time, I only had one other employee.

The morning after I'd returned from an overseas trip to visit family, Larry snapped his Achilles tendon playing basketball and needed immediate surgery. Four days later, there was a blood clot complication.

As he recuperated from his surgery and complications, Larry was unable to walk or move, so I became his arms and legs. During that time, I received a phone call from the North Carolina Highway Patrol informing us that Larry's father, Ralph, had been driving the wrong way on the interstate and caused an accident. Thankfully, no one was seriously hurt, but that day we discovered that Ralph was suffering from the beginning stages of Alzheimer's disease. So I needed to take care of my homebound father-in-law too.

I was still on twenty-four-hour alert to make sure that Larry's blood clot didn't go into his lungs. I was running the business remotely from our home, trying to play catch-up after being out of the office for three weeks. I was also handling all the medical issues for Larry and Ralph.

I felt completely overwhelmed—worried about our money evaporating and terrified of what the next moment held for Larry's health. And how were we going to take care of my father-in-law and manage the business too?

But in the midst of my panic, a calming feeling came over me. I heard these words in my mind: *This is all happening* around *you; it is not happening* to *you.*

In that moment, I experienced a sense of peaceful power. A wave began circling around me. Suspended within this wave were all the difficult situations I was experiencing. I realized that it was true; these things were only happening *around* me. I brought my hands up to my chest and visualized myself pushing the shock wave away. This instantly relieved the heavy pressure on my chest and shoulders and renewed my strength. It kept the present situation from becoming a part of me.

I needed to focus. I needed to remain strong and do what must be done. So I took the steps necessary to make everyone as comfortable and healthy as possible, keep everyone fed, and got everything organized. I kept our clients happy and their work in production. I knew I could do this—I had to do this. There was too much at stake. But I didn't need to be overwhelmed. Everything was happening around me and not happening to me. I had to learn to stop labeling circumstances as good or bad—they simply were what they needed to be at that moment—and to detach myself to prevent becoming emotionally worn down.

For whatever reason, at that moment, I was the one responsible for taking care of these situations as best I could. I believe that a greater "something" was helping me out and helping me to not lose my mind.

There *will* be
lessons and *hardships*
we *must go* through
for *reasons* we may
never know, and from
these *experiences*,
we often *find*
our *level* of
faith grows.

I've often heard that faith can't coexist with fear. I've challenged that concept many times, and I can tell you, from my experience, it stands true. For all of us, it's these difficult times that teach us to rely on faith.

Why Do We Create What We Don't Want?

I've seen the power of what my thoughts and actions can create, both positively and negatively.

We all possess this capability. And it's up to each of us to create the reality we want because no one else can do it for us. At times, I've called this being a "fashioner," a person who gives shape to something new. There will be lessons and hardships we must go through for reasons we may never know, and from these experiences, we often find our level of faith grows. But it also takes deep faith to believe that we can create our own realities. This does not mean we do or don't create all the circumstances around us. We do, however, choose how we participate in them and the attitude we have about them.

There are times when I wonder why I create anything less than awesome in my life. And with all I know about faith and the power of thought, I wonder why fear still shows up to challenge me and try to take over.

Why do we sabotage ourselves with self-defeating actions and negative thoughts? Or as my dear mentor Yvonne would say, "Why do you create crap if you don't want it?"

Maybe we want to become wealthy doing something we love, like creating music or art. Instead of taking action to turn that thought into reality, we tell ourselves we can't possibly make money following our passions. The fact is, it's usually easier to continue doing whatever comes naturally than to work at getting rid of limiting beliefs about ourselves. It seems we've all been effectively conditioned through our families, educations, and the media to know what we can't do.

For instance, how many times do we tell ourselves that we want to triple our businesses but don't ramp up sales, awareness, and marketing efforts to make that happen?

Let's use our wonderful brains to create unlimited possibilities for health, wealth, joy, and love. And then take the actions necessary to create this new reality. It takes action along with faith to produce the results we most want to create. What if we focused on the basics of being healthy and creating a workplace that generates happiness for employees and clients?

It starts with having faith that something bigger than ourselves wants us to create lives and businesses beyond our wildest imaginations. I've learned that we shouldn't get attached to the details of how we'll get there. However, taking multiple actions and paths to make our dreams happen will help the best solution show up in unexpected ways. What? We shouldn't try to micromanage the Universe?

It may take days or years of taking action before that best solution appears. Faith, coupled with action, is how we create success.

So let's stop focusing on all the things we don't have, can't do, or don't want, especially since the Universe seems to just keep giving us what we think about the most.

Why do we *sabotage* ourselves with *self-defeating* actions and negative *thoughts*? Or as my *dear* mentor *Yvonne* would say, "*Wh*y do you *create* crap if you *don't want it*?"

Let's replace those thoughts with infinite possibilities of what we can do incrementally to reach our goals. Take some reflective time to clearly redefine what success—true success—is for you. We don't have to know immediately how we'll get there; we just have to be clear on what that beautiful goal is. Once you reach it, then create the next one. We more than likely won't be able to control the ultimate end goal, so let's create wisely and joyfully along the way.

Full Circle: Framing Your Story

How do you infuse faith into your business?

What's your mindset been during "life swirls?" Would taking on a different perspective help you have more power and be better focused?

If thoughts are things and we can create our own realities, why are you creating things and situations that are less than awesome?

An entrepreneurial brain is fast, jumps all over the place, gets bored easily, or is always creating something. At some point, you must find your focus, remove distractions, and set aside time to check in on your progress.

CHAPTER 12

Focus

Entrepreneurial ADD

Attention deficit disorder (ADD) is a condition that must be diagnosed by a trained mental-health professional through a complete, clinical evaluation.

Entrepreneurial ADD, on the other hand, refers to the characteristics that individuals with ADD often share with the typical entrepreneur: interpersonal skills, grit, energy, passion, creativity, and insight. These traits can be a distinct advantage for entrepreneurs, whether they're actually diagnosed with ADD or not. They're what help many of us business owners successfully launch projects and businesses.

Our entrepreneurial talent for coming up with ideas and solutions may be a blessing, but as a business owner it may also be a curse. The "ideas is what we do" motto works only if we can focus on our ideas long enough to implement, launch, and monetize them. Please don't minimize the negative impact that a lack of focus can have on your life and business.

I deal with the challenge of a bouncing brain that's always searching for ideas to launch a new project. I've recently become aware that I constantly need to be working on a project that consumes me, or I'll fall into a funk. If I deem a challenge too difficult or not creative and fulfilling enough, it's difficult for me to focus on the task. And I'm especially susceptible to distractions if I'm feeling fearful or fatigued. All this makes life difficult for those around me.

My ongoing challenge is segmenting my time so that I can engage in creative projects without sacrificing other parts of my life. For instance, I loved, loved, loved working on the local magazine I launched, but it completely sucked my focus away from everything else. My primary business paid dearly for that.

The ability to search tirelessly for new opportunities, generate tons of business ideas, and maintain an "I can do anything" mindset is fabulous when you're in innovation mode (or the company has grown to the point where your chief role is that of visionary). As an entrepreneurial business owner, we never want to run out of ideas.

However, once your business is launched, it requires a great deal of time and focus. It's impossible to build a long-term, successful business if every bright, shiny, new idea takes you off course.

Let's use our innovative brilliance to create processes, automation, audience awareness, and great teams so that eventually our hands-on involvement isn't needed. It's critical to get one business set up and functioning without us so that we can start the next, and the next, and build a successful empire.

Shiny Opportunities

I'm guilty of getting distracted by bright, shiny objects, which are best described as anything that moves, makes a sound, or crosses my visual field. I keep telling myself that my attention is getting better, but then along comes a distraction.

We all know that business ownership is full of distractions. Dealing with an endless stream of invitations for networking, social events, conferences, and seminar events can deplete our time, energy, and focus. Once I added up the time and money it cost me in a year to attend events and then compared that to the jobs and referrals generated from those events. When I calculated the return on investment, I made a choice to drastically reduce my participation.

There was a two-month stretch during the holidays last year when I could have attended three business events each day. Can you guess how many of those invitations I said yes to?

Zero.

I'll admit that a number of them were tempting, and I felt the guilt of "I probably should" when I declined some of these events. But none of them had the potential to bring money directly into my business. Instead of attending these events, I used my freed-up time to reposition my firm with new marketing materials, help renovate my daughter's house, and write this book. Shiny! (That's for my *Firefly* tribe.)

But I'm not always this strong when it comes to resisting flashy opportunities. If there's an interesting-sounding business lecture, the voice of fear tells me that the presenter must be someone who knows how to do whatever I'm doing better than how I'm doing it. I hate thinking that I'll miss out on an amazing opportunity. But the truth is, most of these shiny situations have nothing to do with what requires my focus at the time. I think the Universe sends them just to test me.

How can you tell if something that comes your way is a real opportunity for you or simply a distraction? Well, I have three quick questions I ask myself whenever I'm in doubt:

1) Is this something I really, really want to do? In other words, will it bring me joy?
2) Is this something that will bring money into my business?
3) Is this something that has the potential to positively impact my business and profit?

If those questions don't settle the issue for you, then here's the final, deciding question: if this event were happening tomorrow, would I drop everything and attend?

If the opportunity/distraction doesn't fall under the category of something I really, really want to do, then it had better positively impact my business by generating profit. I struggled with this idea at first because it seemed to contradict a heart-centered approach. But honestly, I spent too many years doing things that neither impacted my business positively nor brought me joy.

Much of the pro-bono work I've done brought me a great deal of joy. But pro-bono work that became expected rather than appreciated did not, and it didn't provide a return to my business either. For those situations, it makes better sense to write a contribution check instead of using my firm's time to provide free professional services.

The final question is important because if your answer is *not* an "oh, heck, yeah!" then I'd suggest taking a pass. It's way too easy to register for something that is weeks out and hope that your schedule will be less stacked. Keep in mind that you're asking yourself a hypothetical question here, not actually waiting until the last minute to make your decision. I recommend planning events as far ahead as possible in order to create a schedule that works with your energy and to-do list.

Flipping the Focus

Sometimes we need to flip our focus and look at a situation from a different perspective to see a better way.

I'd been working my home-based business for about five years, and my production schedule was over capacity. It was clearly time to move into an office space and hire my first employee.

I gathered my financials and requested a business loan. Unfortunately, I received a series of rejections. My lack of collateral was a factor, but I believe the primary reason my applications were rejected was that the loan officers didn't understand the nature of my business and my need for expansion.

Our *entrepreneurial* talent for *coming up* with ideas and solutions may be a *blessing,* but as a business *owner* it may also *be a curse.*

It was a humbling lesson. I realized that I needed to effectively tell not only my financial story but also my business story. Neither of these stories were fully developed in the initial stages of my business.

There was also a problem with the way I packaged and presented my information. I tried to present like a professional accountant by having super-clean pages of data (lots of numbers) in lieu of a real financial story. But I wasn't an accountant; I was a designer, and my firm produced beautiful, colorful magazines and promotional materials, not spreadsheets.

It was time to flip the focus. I took the time to redo my presentation and recreate my business plan, financials, and loan request. I presented my story the way I would for a client.

I was still turned down by five banks, but the sixth one, Bank of America, wrote me a check for everything I requested. That gave me the safety net I needed for my first expansion. Changing my focus made all the difference.

From my designer days, I have a trick I use if something doesn't look right and I can't figure out why it isn't working. I print it out and stand across the room and look at the design in a mirror. Moving farther from the project and seeing it reversed gives me a totally new viewpoint.

Likewise, when we have a specific business challenge, we can flip our perspectives by asking a friend, stranger, or networking colleague for their point of view on the matter. Keep

Sometimes we need to *flip* our *focus* and *look* at a situation from a *different perspective* to see a *better way*.

in mind that everyone has opinions, and you'll need to sort out the ones that are most appropriate. I've found that with this process, someone will invariably ask a question that topples my current theory and offers a brand-new frame of reference. This has the power to completely flip my focus on the situation.

Focus Check-ins

What should we be focusing on in our businesses? Well, first we need to understand the difference between vision and goals. "Vision" is the impact each of us desires to make on our world or industries or communities. It is also a key part of the roadmap to where we want our businesses and ourselves to arrive. It's like the GPS (global positioning system) address we plug into our map apps. It's frequently written in the present tense as though it's already happened. Our goals then are the rest of the map—the necessary steps that take us toward our visions. If you haven't clearly articulated your vision, it will be seriously difficult to focus and even more difficult to arrive at your destination.

We often focus on specific business goals that help us make short-term progress and get our plans started. But then we must set up processes to generate progress toward our goals. Focusing on, and documenting, a process creates long-term results.

Setting goals can often feel like trying to predict the future. Our unmet expectations can lead to disappointment or feelings of failure. I've set many goals with the expectation of a certain outcome unfolding in a certain way within a certain time frame. Either I didn't take the actions that were required to make those goals happen, or it wasn't the right time and circumstance. And most often the goal didn't happen because it wasn't part of a grander vision and because I tried to micromanage the outcome. (I now fondly call this micromanaging the Universe.) When we create a goal, it must be part of a vision. Taking action and moving forward brings forth resources and opportunities, many of which we may not have been able to see as options. Once the vision is clear, we must surrender the details and the specifics of how we want our businesses' visions to come true. How we get there may be quite fluid or bumpy with important detours and delays that strengthen our experience and knowledge. Nonetheless, keep moving forward toward the vision. Keeping your vision clear is very important. Make yourself available for coincidences and small miracles along the way.

So stay true to your vision or destination, but don't become attached to the path, direction, or mile markers to get there. Those may change in ways we never could have imagined or planned.

Just because we plan or work to create something, it simply may not happen as we wanted or in the timing that we expected. Then all we can control is how we react to it. And perhaps "try, try again" with various different perspectives to get clearer on the vision.

When it comes to achieving goals toward my vision, I've learned to focus my energy on the process for progress. When I'm most focused, I schedule fifteen minutes each Friday to fill out a quick feedback grid to track my progress (filling it in daily helps tremendously). It's a simple review that provides helpful feedback and discoveries. For example, this practice has helped me realize that I wanted to increase referrals, but I wasn't scheduling enough intentional interactions, meetings, or opportunities to make that happen. Or I needed to increase my energy to manage the awesome projects I wanted to add into my business, yet I wasn't silencing my mind or exercising daily to increase energy levels.

The feedback grid helps me identify the five key things I must do on a weekly basis to achieve the results I'm seeking in my business. I chose to do this every Friday because it's another fabulous *F* word and rounds out the workweek.

It's amazing what we can learn about ourselves when we document and track our progress. Focusing on this feedback provides clarity and insight. Download a sample of my feedback grid at FabiPreslar.com/resources.

Full Circle: Framing Your Story

Will the professional event you're considering attending bring joy, opportunity, or profit to your business?

Are you willing to document and measure your weekly progress?

Have you created action steps to get you toward the goal you're focusing on?

Learn how to be heart-driven in your team's culture, yet monitor your expectations so as not to cross over too far into the personal space and never into the friend space.

CHAPTER 13

Fabric

Employees Are the Threads

My employees are the strength of my firm. Building my team has been among my biggest challenges in growing my business and has resulted in a number of personal and professional lessons.

The following stories may make you question how anyone can be as sensitive or pathetic or ignorant as I was. Well, my inner circle of family and friends are deeply important to me. Too often I blurred the line between friends and employees and responded to my emotions instead of focusing on building a talented team with a great culture. This involves a healthy degree of detachment and a clear company-growth strategy. I've learned to let go of expectations and relinquish control. Most importantly, I've stopped taking personal responsibility for my employees reaching their potentials or rather what I identified as their potentials.

If building your team is not something you struggle with, then congratulations on this accomplishment. It took me a long time, lots of energy, and more than a little heartbreak to get there.

Saving the World, One Employee at a Time

Most of the problems I've had with personnel stemmed from me being uninformed. Despite my lack of business sense, I always meant well.

As the business grew, I felt a universal duty to help people. Armed with my limited business knowledge and my limited power on Earth, I set out on a mission to change the world, one employee at a time. My objective was to provide a workplace where folks could heal and grow. My intention was to find employees with potential and give them a space to blossom.

Warning: be careful what you ask for. The Universe responded by bringing a stream of personally burdened folks to my doorstep. There are lots of dysfunctional people with untapped potential out there, and that's exactly who I attracted and hired. It was difficult to get high-level work done in between the drama and tears, situation after situation. I had quite a bit of turnover as I worked to build a healthy, productive team.

I've retained employee assistance programs, counselors, and consultants to assist members of my team as they struggled with various life challenges. Each and every one of them had talent, but it was overshadowed by their personal problems. As a business owner, I had difficulty getting them to be profitable. A successful creative company can't function with that much drama. I grew physically and emotionally exhausted.

I went to one of my guides and described the broken lives and painful situations within my team. I was tired of running an emotional day care, and shouldering that burden was more than I could bear. Then my guide asked this question: "Why did you choose such a team, and why did you choose to run an emotional daycare if that's not what you want to do?"

This question, of course, made me angry. What did I do that was so wrong? I was just following my heart. I was trying to give everyone an opportunity to share their talent and reach their potential.

And that was the problem. It was time for me to rethink my company's mission. Who was it I really wanted to serve? My employees' personal lives or my business and my clients?

Answering that question was a turning point for me. I remembered whom I built my company to serve and shifted my focus to serving the client first with exceptional talent. In doing so, my firm provides a space for employees to grow personally and creatively. It was a gradual change that took place over eighteen months. The new mission formed the basis for each new hire.

It's been a beautiful thing to see this change in action, but it took some hard lessons to get where we are. I'd wanted to manage my firm through heart-centered leadership, but hiring folks whom I thought I could help was not leadership. Leading from the heart doesn't mean getting walked over by others or taking on their personal issues.

Your Employees Are Not Your Friends

Over the course of my childhood and career, I've created a tough outer shell for survival. It's my way of protecting my mushy why-can't-we-all-get-along-and-love-each-other insides.

Business ownership has taught me numerous lessons about employees and friendships. Sadly, I've not been a quick study, and many of these experiences still hurt when I think about them. I'll briefly share a few and point out the error of my ways, just so you won't repeat my mistakes.

Awkward Manager. In one of the departments I managed after my exit from my first business, my role was to restructure the department. Everyone had to reinterview for their job, which unsurprisingly didn't go over well with employees. I reported to the owner of the company, and together we selected the remaining team.

Unfortunately, the person who was the least qualified for her position in the revamped department was the favorite of the group (of course). I did my job and let her go. I then had to deal with the team's retaliation. The group made a show of not including me in conversations or anything social. Their behavior made for many awkward moments in the office.

For instance, my husband had sent me flowers and a Mylar balloon for my birthday. Anyone who knows me understands that my birthday is an important day for me. The team gathered outside my office door, talking loudly about plans for lunch. They shot me a final look as they were leaving, just to drive home the fact that my birthday balloon and I were not invited.

I determined then and there that I'd never have employees like that in my own business. I would create a workplace culture in which this kind of high-school mentality was not an option. I wanted to be a strong manager and lead with heart and no drama.

The First Cut Is the Deepest. My first full-time employee took a long time to recruit. I had pulled him away from another position and felt a huge sense of responsibility in even promising him a full year of employment. Training him took many months, but I couldn't get him profitable. Break even, yes, but profitable, no.

I struggled to decide whether I should keep him on board. I wanted to honor my promise, but it wasn't making sense to do so. Throughout our conversations, he shared a great deal about his life and mentioned that at some point he'd like to move back to the mountains.

I made the decision to let him go. It was difficult enough firing an employee at someone else's company, but this was the first time I'd had to fire my own employee. I was devastated. I felt not only an overwhelming sense of failure but also regret for having broken a promise. Plus, I'd need to pay increased unemployment fees. I cried as I let him go. He hugged me and told me it was OK and that everything was going to be fine.

Building a
talented team with
a *great culture*
involves a *healthy* degree
of *detachment*
and a *clear*
company-growth
strategy.

When I was cleaning up his desk and email account after he left, I discovered emails detailing his plans to move to the mountains. He was all set to move within two weeks. Just two weeks! He would have resigned, and I wouldn't be paying for unemployment or feeling like I'd broken a promise.

This taught me to never make promises during negotiations or guarantee a length of employment. Everything is dependent on the employee's performance and profitability.

I also learned that even though we shared many pleasant conversations, my employee wasn't my friend, and he wasn't going to divulge his personal plans. Another lesson in hindsight is that there's a time and a place for everyone. He wasn't the right person for the next phase of my business. My firm wasn't the right place for him to be for the next phase of his life. He went on to blossom and create a wonderful new life and career. I've since stopped making every employee transition so personal.

Allow me to put it *bluntly*: the folks you *manage* and *provide paychecks* for *are not* your *friends*, they're your *employees*.

Diva on Board. After reorganizing my team with my new mission, one employee remained from the "save the world one employee at a time" era. She was my greatest employee challenge ever.

My biggest mistake was truly caring about her and her continually difficult circumstances. I made sacrifices for her regularly and tolerated behavior that was not acceptable within a professional environment. Why? Because letting her go during her present life crisis would have made me feel like a horrible human being. Instead, I created all sorts of work-arounds.

I finally made the decision to let her go at the end of the year, which was five months away. During that time, she wore down the team and sunk morale to an all-time low. I invested a great many resources in her well-being and even enrolled her in a program to help recharge her own spirit and creativity. But the tears and diva outbursts continued.

My husband had organized a party for me for an upcoming mile-marker birthday. The event was being held an hour after one of our business events at the same location. (The venue was paid for a full day, so why not?) She was the first employee to say she wanted to be there. I decided to bend my rule and invited my entire team.

When weekly timesheets were turned in for that week, she essentially logged the event as overtime. That was quite a wake-up call for me of her personality. When she quit less than thirty days later, her exit, if filmed, could have won a theatrical award.

It just goes to show that, at times, good people in the wrong situation can bring out a less-than-great version of each person involved. She is now thriving in a better-suited environment for her, and our culture has fabulously readjusted.

Another lesson that became clear: if I've weighed all the facts and made the decision to let someone go, then I need to let them go immediately. I've often invested more time and more resources to help one member of my team gain better skills or to give them more time to prove their talent. But when I've had that gut feeling they were not a fit, delaying the inevitable has never worked in my favor. The practice I now work with is to hire slow and fire fast (if the employee is not a fit).

Allow me to put it bluntly: the folks you manage and provide paychecks for are not your friends; they're your employees. I know plenty of colleagues who thought of their employees as friends, but when they sold their companies, their former employees never returned their calls and cancelled planned get-togethers. The relationship ended the minute the paychecks ended. It's not about being unlikeable or heartless; it's about being clear on your boundaries and creating better relationships than pal-like friendships with your team.

Weaving a Fine Fabric

Employees provide the core fabric of my business. Together, we can build a healthy, vibrant, and heart-centered culture. I provide my team with creative space, effective tools, and cool projects. In exchange for that and receiving their paychecks, the team wows our clients with inventive solutions that generate profit and increase the value of our firm.

These creative collaborations are more valuable than friendships. Together, we can serve a high-level client whose mission is to make a positive difference in our world. We get to see our magazine and catalog designs distributed throughout the country and around the globe. And the custom books that we're creating for our clients are impacting lives and businesses in meaningful ways, as well as winning awesome national awards for our clients.

Beyond happy clients and growing profits, I'm not sure what your barometer is to know you have a beautiful fabric within your culture. A definite highlight for me was when I recently overheard part of my team proudly share that they were part of our family. What an amazing way to spend our workdays, with my family and work family weaved together. It was worth doing all the humbling work to reach this point.

We bring our past experiences into our businesses. Our company histories, clients, and employees are great teachers. As business owners, we need to be receptive to these lessons and weave what we've learned into the fabric of our companies.

Full Circle: Framing Your Story

Is each person in your company in the right seat and sharing valuable, profitable talent?

Are you mucking up the culture of your company with your own past knowledge?

Are you leading a heart-centered culture within your company? How do you know? How does your team know?

Remove the social illusion that lack of sleep equals success. Make time both for sleep and restful silence to help you recharge and quiet your mind.

CHAPTER 14

Fatigue

Sleep Is Your Friend

didn't used to sleep much. I'd grown up hearing that sleeping was for lazy people, and I had a mentor who believed that sleeping more than four hours every night was a waste of a good life.

In college, I worked three jobs and carried a full course load and always seemed to have design projects due. I remember that one time I wanted to visit an out-of-town friend for the weekend. The only way I could make that happen was by sleeping for only two hours each night that week. As you can imagine, that weekend was disastrous. I couldn't function. But I was eighteen years old, so no lessons were learned. I kept right on crossing sleep off of my schedule to make room for more life.

My idea that sleep is optional persisted throughout the years that I was making weekly trips to care for my mentor, Yvonne, and working to move my new business beyond the startup stage. I slept very little, if at all, during my two-day visits with Yvonne. Fatigue often caught up with me and created scary moments during my two-hour drive back home on the interstate. It's another way I know there are angels.

I was so exhausted during that period that I once fell asleep mid-sentence while talking to my daughter. It was the middle of the afternoon, and she feared that I'd died right in front of her. At the time, I was getting wicked migraines from overexertion and lack of sleep.

I worked ridiculously long days at my business. I'd postscript the files for large magazines and take a series of two-hour naps while the files processed. Then I'd set up the next step and sleep the next two hours. I'd repeat the process throughout the night. Meanwhile, my days were spent designing and speaking with clients.

My friend Bonnie is an amazingly productive woman who works in contract sales. She is a fireball of energy. I finally asked her how she had so much energy. Her secret, she said, was making sure she slept a minimum of eight hours each night. I'd never heard of anyone doing that. This shattered the belief that I'd lived by for years. Bonnie was far from lazy. She was always kind and pleasant and accomplished more each day than most business people I knew.

I'm forever grateful to Bonnie for giving me permission to be a successful person who makes sleep a priority. I now sleep eight hours every night and take a nap on the weekend when it works out. My husband is an expert weekend napper and has trained me well.

I know how to pack a remarkable number of tasks into a workweek. So on a day off, or on the weekend after I've had a particularly "peopley" week, I may lay in bed after my eight hours and read or sleep a bit more. And I do so without thinking awful things about myself.

On occasion, I still call myself lazy, but I now know I'm the only one who would.

A business *owner's thoughts* never stop. We're *constantly* planning, *thinking*, linking, strategizing, *creating*, and *seeking*. With that much activity in *our brains*, *we need* a daily dose of *silence*. Otherwise, our *circuits can overload.*

Self-Care

I pushed and worked hard to grow my business, but I did so at the expense of my health. My body was young and resilient, but eventually it started showing signs of abuse. I could go days and weeks without proper sleep and nourishment until, slowly but surely, I couldn't.

In the throes of working long days and evenings in my home-based business, I'd had a breast cyst scare. The test results were inconclusive after the lumpectomy. But I counted my blessings: no radiation or ongoing treatments were necessary.

A few years later, I was working long and hard in my first office and couldn't seem to stabilize my energy. I was diagnosed as pre-diabetic (though I wasn't overweight) and put on medication. This convinced me to begin focusing on my health, and within two years of changing my diet, I was off the medication.

Migraines and fibroids continued to present physical challenges, but nothing slowed me like having to undergo two major surgeries within nine months. I wasn't sure I was going to be human after that. Thanks to medical science, I did indeed remain human and seemed, in fact, to be thriving. But then came the shocking, terrifying prospect of needing a third surgery. At that point, I finally made it my highest priority to value and honor my body.

Hindsight reveals that most of my health issues could have been avoided. Stress and fatigue fry our bodies, and unhealthy food and drink act as toxins. Every one of us is given a body bank, and each time we abuse our bodies, our currency dwindles.

If you want to succeed in business, a healthy vehicle (your body) needs to drive that business. This requires regular, radical self-care. Unfortunately, we rarely listen to our bodies until they scream out in pain or simply shut down.

My diet now consists of clean, mostly organic foods: lean meats, whole grains, fruits, and vegetables. I prefer savory over sweet, so my sugar intake is limited. Caffeine wrecks my nervous system and makes my brain hyper. However, I do enjoy a chai latte on occasion. My team insists that I announce when I've had one, so they can prepare for the onslaught of emails detailing my numerous requests and brilliant suggestions. Removing stress and fear have been my biggest challenges, but I'm learning to reduce and reroute this toxic energy. And I continue to work on ways to consistently incorporate exercise into my daily routine.

Take a Walk

When I get tired, I'm much less able to resist whatever I'm trying to resist. Have you ever experienced that "too tired to fight it" feeling?

When I need an attitude adjustment, my best remedy is to take a walk. It gives me time to think without distraction and is my favorite go-to activity. The fresh air fills my lungs, and I'm able to breathe in a new perspective. I usually walk on a quiet, wooded park trail or in my neighborhood where there are lots of trees and wooded lots.

I love going for long walks with my husband. Sometimes there are long silences. Other times, we cut up and talk about silly things. Or we find ourselves talking strategy about the business. Often, Larry calms me down about some business concern I have by sharing his unique outlook on the same situation. We have similar value systems but tend to see things quite differently.

No matter what the day has had in store for me, I always feel better after taking a walk.

Recharge

Sleep is nightly; self-care and the practice of silence are daily. All help ward off fatigue. Even with those priorities in place, I find that after prolonged periods of time focusing on business and the challenges of daily life, a recharge is needed.

For me, a recharge is stepping away from my everyday routine for a change of scenery and new stimuli. Or no stimuli. There are short recharges and long recharges. One of my favorite long recharges is renting a house on the beach with a covered balcony, so my husband and I can be beach bums for ten full days. I love keeping vacation time simple and unscheduled, with no people or obligations. We eat simply and sleep, walk, nap, read, and walk, then sit, stare, and walk some more. It can sometimes take four or five days before we're able to release the obligations of the office and completely decompress.

I have friends who schedule two consecutive weeks every business quarter to unwind. I know other business owners who take a minimum of four weeks at a time to travel. I aspire to having this kind of time away from the office, but I'm not yet there.

I should add that I truly love my business and working. These times away aren't to escape but to get a renewed outlook and to recharge and recreate (or "re-create"). This is especially important since my husband and I work, live, and play together.

Beyond the recharge, there are other benefits to stepping away. We clear a space in our cluttered minds for new ideas and perspectives. Our delegation skills become much better, and we more fully appreciate the skills and capabilities of our team. What a joy it is to discover that our employees can handle things quite well in our absence. Time away from the daily operations has also helped me identify changes that needed to be made to strengthen the team.

Of course, a weekly recharge of a day or two off is mandatory. Dan Sullivan, founder of Strategic Coach, requires that his students completely shut down for a full twenty-four hours each week. That means no checking emails, texts, or voicemails, and no calling into the office.

We *simply* do not
operate at *peak efficiency*
when we put in a
fifty-plus *hour workweek*
or don't properly
manage our energy.

How different would our businesses and we be if this recharge were part of our weekly practice? We simply do not operate at peak efficiency when we put in a fifty-plus hour workweek or don't properly manage our energy.

Silence

Whether this means setting aside time for reflection or practicing meditation, being in silence helps me reduce the level of clutter in my mind and makes me more efficient during the day. I take time in the morning for silence. For me, meditation is processing a new concept and letting it sink in during stillness. I allow thoughts and questions to grow during the coming days. It's also a time for me to plant a mental seed or intention and then release it. It's a challenge to simply watch things unfold. The answers come, problems are resolved, and opportunities show up.

A business owner's thoughts never stop. We're constantly planning, thinking, linking, strategizing, creating, and seeking. With that much activity in our brains, we need a daily dose of silence. Otherwise, our circuits can overload.

Every one of us is given a *body bank,* and each time *we abuse* our bodies, *our currency dwindles.*

Full Circle: Framing Your Story

What is your belief
about sleep, and what
is your sleep routine?

How do you recharge?
Is it working?

What is your self-care
process for success?

What would it take to
make silence an important
part of your day?

What have you learned from
the last few times you were
sick, hurt, or unwell? What
do you think your body
was trying to say to you?

Sometimes a bad experience fosters a good one. You figure things out as you go along and when the timing is right. Just remember the lessons, so it's easier next time. If a process is the result, document it.

CHAPTER 15

Foster

Transforming along the Way

I f you aren't growing, you aren't living. For me, the process of transformation involves chipping away at layers of self and ego. Each lesson learned fosters and encourages further development. And yes, this is as painful as it sounds. However, the long-term payoff is worth the short-term pain.

There are traumatic situations that cause us to transform, and there are simple moments that define us. Sometimes, the pain leaves marks that last a lifetime. The situations that lead to transformation can leave trauma in our cells and in our subconscious.

One of those defining moments happened to me as a young child. I remember being scared of a big, deep swimming pool. There were people all around, but then suddenly, my father picked me up and hurled me into the water. I heard him shout the word, "Swim!" I had no idea how to swim, but I knew I'd better figure something out pretty quickly because I couldn't breathe! This was the moment I learned that there will be many things in life I don't know how to do, but I'm entirely capable of jumping in and figuring it out.

Two contrasting experiences with launching a magazine brought this lesson home for me once again. The first launch floundered but fostered ideas for how to make another attempt successful.

True Colors

I'd always wanted to launch and publish my own magazine as a creative outlet.

Years ago, I saw a need for a magazine tailored to the affluent lifestyle of the racing community. I shared the idea with a man who ran a new sales-networking club. I didn't know him well, but at the time, I put my faith in folks I believed were smarter than me, which back then included almost everyone I met. I trusted his sales expertise, and we began having deeper conversations about the processes and steps to launch the magazine. He was supportive and mentioned tons of potential contacts and resources from his network as possible advertisers. We discussed a long-range plan and the steps needed to begin this project.

Once he'd gathered the information from our conversations, he drew up a contract with his lawyer buddy and, without my knowledge, went directly to the client. The client then signed a contract for his company to own and launch the magazine.

When I told him that I was drawing up the contract, he let me know he'd already "locked in the client" and all I had to do was sign. He'd be handling things directly. It was difficult to rein in my temper, especially when I found out that he'd also assigned himself the role of publisher. But he told me not to worry, that I'd still be the one to create the content, design the overall look, produce the pages, and work with the editors and photographers. I'd have complete creative freedom. He had not only thrown me into the deep end with no warning but also stolen my entire hamburger and just flipped me the pickles.

I felt defeated, but I eventually came to the conclusion that this was still an opportunity to create an exciting new publication, and I accepted the deal. The fact was, this man had money to bring into this project, and I did not; in my mind, that gave him all the power. I let him know that because he owned the magazine, he'd be responsible for paying the vendors directly.

The first issue launched with a bang and high media attention. The second issue was underway, with several more big-dollar advertisers coming in. I was managing the writers, photographers, and editors. He'd paid me for the first issue, and I assumed everyone else had been paid too. The concept was great, and the magazine appeared to be successful, so the vendors all wanted to be part of it. None of them mentioned that they hadn't been paid.

But as the second issue went to the printer, everything went silent on the man's end. He had pocketed all the money from both issues without paying any of the vendors and then disappeared. None of that money was ever recouped, and my relationships with the vendors were forever damaged.

In retrospect, I believe this man read my inexperience like a neon sign on my forehead. I was guilty of wearing rose-colored glasses, and I've since learned that we need clear vision to see people's true colors. A taker is a thief. Expecting the best of a taker is like trying to save a hurt cobra; it will get what it needs, then strike you when it can.

As business owners, we must be and stay observant. These days, a red flag, such as a nervous twitch, a shifting of the eyes, or an unmet commitment will sound off my alert system to begin asking further questions. This helps me identify people who will be valuable partners, people whose purpose is to succeed with me instead of taking advantage of me.

I Can See Clearly Now

As awful as that initial magazine experience was, the lessons it provided were golden. I'd proved to myself that I had the necessary tools and know-how to launch and run a magazine.

I've been approached three times to either buy or partner with someone to own an existing magazine. Thanks to my lawyer and CPA, I know how to exercise initial due diligence and exactly who to call to help me review client books, contracts, assets, and the opted-in/subscribed audience.

When I reviewed each opportunity, I put away my rose-colored glasses, so I could see the situation realistically. I immersed myself in the idea for a few days, imagining what it would feel like to be in that role and what level of time, resources, and commitments it would take.

I eventually turned down all of the offers because each one had a specific aspect I wasn't willing to take on. I'll admit that I cried each time, but interestingly enough, none of those publications are currently in business.

Over the years, I've bought names and URLs for several original magazine concepts that I've had. All of them were based on showcasing inspiring stories of everyday people. By delving into each concept and assessing what the magazine might look and feel like and whom it would serve, I often discovered I wasn't the right person to create it. I "live" an idea before I take any steps toward launching it.

There's a fair amount of intuition and assumption that goes into my concept immersion process. I take my time and imagine a number of different paths and directions and allow them to shift and change. I need to be completely in tune with my body's reaction to each of them. When a certain path feels right, I feel a sense of joy, along with terror and excitement. Then I know I can start taking steps toward my vision. These steps may include list-making and a series of detours before I actually get to the fun and real part.

There are *traumatic* situations that cause us to *transform*, and there are *simple* moments that *define us.*

I should note that in addition to the above listed emotions, I typically experience some degree of resistance. This resistance is typically my insecurity and laziness. There are countless details that go along with launching a project or new business, and this inconvenience doesn't always sit well with the side of me that often fears failure and would prefer to not complicate life. But at the same time, my creative, entrepreneurial side is shouting, "Woohoo! Let's make this dream happen!"

Timing

Eventually, my vision for creating a magazine for local business owners became clear. I secured a national trademark registration for the name and logo. The content, manifesto, themes, and direction of the magazine followed effortlessly. My team designed the nameplate, and I felt ready to launch my dream magazine.

Then came a series of blocks.

I'd lined up an awesome salesperson with superpowers in our local community. With her talent I knew we could afford a top-notch editor, writers, and photographers. But the day before we were to finalize our agreement, her husband's job required them to move out of state. I was forced to put plans on hold.

I also realized I couldn't generate enough revenue for the top-notch business magazine editor I'd hoped to hire. I continued to delay the project, which meant that I had to pay fines and file extensions with the national registration board.

In addition, my in-house writer/editor left the firm to go back to school for her master's degree. I knew that I needed to ratchet up the talent a few notches with a powerhouse communications person for the next position.

Clearly, there were too many issues going on within the business for me to be dreaming of a passion project.

Then out of the blue, a long-time magazine editor client responded to my job ad. I thought it was a mistake. But she said that she was impressed with the culture of my firm and the high-quality creative work we produced, and she wanted to be part of the team. I already had a solid candidate and was blown away to have a second strong option. After two more tough interview rounds, I offered the position to her. Based on previous projects, I knew we could collaborate well. And based on asking the right questions, I knew she would honor my vision and ownership of the magazine.

The blocks keeping this project from moving forward were now gone. Together, she and I created a brilliant concept of a magazine called *b2bTRIBE*. My husband and our creative team poured their extraordinary creative and photographic talents into the project. Our first issue even won a national magazine competition as best new business-to-business magazine in the country!

The magazine went on to win ten regional and national awards for its overall concept, writing, and design. It also contributed to me winning several entrepreneurial awards, as well as the B2B Marketer of the Year from the Business Marketing Association of the Carolinas.

Because we had few resources to produce this magazine, we learned to develop ingenious automated solutions to reduce the amount of staff needed.

For example, there was no money to hire a salesperson or additional editors and writers, so we created a content portal to help crowdsource (meaning we invited readers to contribute) and curate the content, as well as an advertising portal to automate the purchasing and uploading of ads. I had the vision, and my team designed the technology to make that vision a reality. It was all developed in-house by our talented communications director and my brilliant husband, our creative director—a true team effort.

We published six issues of this stellar magazine over the course of three years and hosted three exclusive sold-out events for local business owners. No other project in my career has challenged the concept of "figuring it out" to this level and yet provided me with such a great sense of personal satisfaction.

Every idea, situation, or dream you have may not clearly unfold in front of you with all the available resources. Sometimes the opportunity is the process to create and innovate along the way. I got to see and value our communications director even more and got to celebrate her and my team's innovative ideas through this project. It set the tone for future projects (of which there will be many). It revealed a level of confidence in my team and me. So don't be afraid to foster the opportunities you do have and forge ahead as you figure things out along the way; just don't forget the lessons previously learned and see how they can all be packaged together.

Full Circle: Framing Your Story

Are you looking at business opportunities with rose-colored glasses? Are they keeping you from seeing a reality in front of you?

Do you ever feel a "block" that's holding back progress? Could it be that the right time hasn't arrived?

Have you overlooked a possible resource?

Every *idea, situation*, or *dream* you have may not clearly *unfold* in front of you with *all* the available *resources*. Sometimes the *opportunity* is the process to *create* and *innovate along the way*.

Networking is neither foolproof nor one-size-fits-all. You may have some awkward interactions. Don't waste energy worrying about those. Focus on interactions that benefit your business.

CHAPTER 16

Fraternizing

The Social Beehive

Small business ownership protocol seems to require networking in order for us to stay locally relevant and connected by attending numerous luncheons, dinners, and presentations. Beyond offering opportunities to network and to meet vendor partners and potential referrals, these events have been catalysts for personal growth. They seem to have a way of shining a spotlight on insecurities.

The complexity of networking is perceived quite differently for most of my male and female business owner friends. The perception and process also varies depending on whether you are an introvert or extrovert. An introvert may feel like they have to hold their breath while running the gauntlet, while an extrovert in the exact same situation may feel they are walking into a fun festival of people.

I cannot share the experience from an extrovert's viewpoint. However, as I share some of my encounters, I get very different feedback. An extroverted man read this chapter and said to take it out of this book—it was unnecessary and made me sound weak. How fortunate for him that he doesn't understand or relate to this chapter. However, when introverted women read this chapter, their response was, "OMG, those things happen to you too?!" Quite a few have shared they completely relate and have their own unique experiences with networking.

For an introvert, networking takes a huge amount of energy and focus. Amongst all the camaraderie and deal making, we're surrounded by people with big smiles and go-get-'em attitudes, all seeking a way to be memorable.

For me, these events often feel like being inside a beehive. Everyone in the hive has a role. Some attendees are worker bees who buzz about meeting people and exchanging pleasantries. Often, they don't follow up afterward. Then there are the energetic, salesy bees who keep the event humming. They are ready and eager to learn more about your business and explain their own, and they will most likely follow up promptly to schedule a coffee date.

Then there's the occasional, stealthy, stinger bee. I never seem to see them coming, but they pack a zinger of a sting that can knock an unsuspecting networker off guard.

I've met thousands of people at hundreds of events and on dozens of committees just to get a seat at a few tables and have folks remember my name. Networking takes a great deal of intentional work: smiling, shaking hands, exchanging business cards, following up, showing up, and taking action. On a good day, when I'm feeling confident and have had enough sleep, I can navigate a networking event fairly well.

A great deal of good can come from purposeful networking. For me, it has brought on some additional unexpected social lessons. You'd think that after twenty-plus years of intentional networking, I'd have learned most of the lessons that fraternizing has to teach. But nope! On occasion, a stealthy bee stings me just at the right time.

Some folks
don't "stir" well.
We need to save
transparent moments
and probing *questions*
for *our closest* circle
of *colleagues* or
our *coaching* and
strategy clients.

Being Stung

I had the privilege of being invited to a private luncheon with about fifty leading ladies to celebrate an influential friend and mentor. I was one of her newer friends, but she'd been friends with many of the women in attendance for forty-plus years. Unlike me, most of the guests were very wealthy. The event was held in a beautiful room at the Duke Mansion.

I had just placed my purse on a seat at the front table when an elegant older woman across the room recognized me. I walked over to say hello, and she invited me to join her table. I pointed to the front of the room where my purse was placed, and as I started to explain, she tilted her head, touched my arm, and in a slow Southern drawl said, "Oh, you're working this event."

Her words were a knife that cut into the raw insecurity I've always felt when among elite women. I felt the familiar pain of being "less than" or "not worthy." I knew the hurt of being treated like I had no right to be there.

Fortunately, our dear, gracious host was gathering everyone to their seats to begin the festivities. So I lifted my head, put on my best networking smile, and marched to my seat.

Now, this older woman didn't knowingly plunge that dagger into me. I have no idea what she meant by her comment. All I know is the unresolved feelings that it triggered. After the lunch, I drove back to my office, replaying a dark movie in my head. It was an old, classic movie, rereleased with that single, short sentence.

I've since resolved those feelings. I understand that I was invited into that lovely room because I did belong, or I wouldn't have been there. Yes, it was unfortunate that this woman assumed that I wouldn't sit with her because I was "working the event." At that moment, I heard her say I was hired help. But to be fair, I was hired help in restaurants for many years and still, in fact, work for my clients. I just didn't happen to be on the clock in service mode at that particular moment.

Several months later, I once again crossed paths with the woman at a reception. She was leaving but stopped briefly to share a kind word with me. She asked if I was part of the Women Presidents' Organization. I said that I wasn't but hoped to be in the near future. She smiled and said, "We'll have to see what we can do about that," and told me she'd see me later.

Walking behind her was her beautiful husband who walked very slowly. He appeared to have had a mild stroke, which dimmed his light. This woman in all her power was shining a light for both of them. Yet she graciously took a moment to stop and ask me a relevant question. I keep this example as a social bookmark. The experiences I shared with this woman brought me three valuable lessons.

We never know what someone is thinking. Some statements, especially during networking or business events, are made impulsively. Sometimes they mean something; sometimes they don't. People who make hurtful comments may be nervous or in a hyped-up networking mode, unable to connect their thoughts. Maybe they have us confused with someone else. Or maybe an angel has jumped into their heads to teach us lessons we need to learn.

We tote our baggage everywhere. When we carry past hurts, insecurities, and judgments around, they quickly lead us to jump to assumptions and conclusions that are very much a reflection of our inner beliefs, insecurities, and conversations. An unresolved past can color every situation. Think about the colorful chaos of a social event where everyone experiences a single situation completely differently based on their own interpretations. Now that you are thinking about it, how could it happen any other way?

We never know what someone is going through. We tend to forget this. Why do we insist on making everything about us? Every single person is going through "something." It could be as simple as a headache or as serious as a loved one's terminal illness. Our current circumstances change our states of mind.

Who Has the Dagger?

Imagine being the person who said something that accidentally cut into someone's deep emotions. You see the pained look on that person's face but have no idea what just happened.

I was once the one wielding the dagger at a women's dinner. I'm not clear what the lesson was for the young woman who was cut by my comment, but I learned several valuable lessons for myself.

Prior to this incident, we'd met one another but had never had a complete conversation. The awkward moment came when another colleague asked the two of us if we'd met before. In response, the woman began repeatedly bowing toward me. I lightly touched her arm and asked what she was doing. She said she was "bowing down to the fabulous Fabi Preslar."

This struck me as weird and totally unwarranted. When I expressed something to that effect, her eyes filled with tears, and her face reddened. She threw her hands up and excused herself to race to the restroom.

My colleague and I stood there quite confused. Had we both missed something? After a few minutes, I decided to go check on her. I apologized for whatever I'd said that upset her. But instead of my apology calming her down, it enraged her. She started yelling at me about how this was not the time and place for this conversation. There was no logic to her words. She went back into the main room and ranted to everyone who crossed her path.

When I apologized to her again, she broke down and said she was awaiting a diagnosis and she'd had a long, trying day. Then she left.

The rest of the meeting was informative, and I shook off this bizarre incident. But as soon as I returned home, I wrote the woman a brief, kind email about her impending diagnosis and wished her the best in whatever challenges were ahead. I sent a wave of love to her and launched the email. Her reply

When *we carry* past hurts, *insecurities,* and *judgments* around, they quickly lead *us to jump* to assumptions and *conclusions* that are very much a *reflection* of our *inner beliefs*, insecurities, and *conversations.*

came back immediately stating: "And here I thought you were reaching out to apologize."

As uncalled for as this encounter was, I needed to be accountable for my part. But once logic left the conversation, I dropped it. (I later found out that her diagnosis was OK, by the way).

We don't need to be open and transparent with everyone. The more public we become, the more important it is to remain gracious but to avoid stirring things up by asking questions or offering comments to those we don't know. Some folks don't "stir" well. We need to save transparent moments and probing questions for our closest circle of colleagues or our coaching and strategy clients.

Don't waste precious energy on people who will not appreciate it. As soon as we realize someone is on a different wavelength, we need to let the topic go. No matter how well intentioned our words may be, they may not be accurately heard or interpreted. Save your grace and move on.

Don't be a fixer. I had already observed that, for whatever reason, there was a divide of some sort with this woman. I should have gone with my gut and left the situation alone. Instead, I attempted to try to fix it.

I share these anecdotes not for the actual incidents but for the lessons I later extracted from them and for the understanding that any one of us could be on either side of an awkward situation.

As we gain more experience and more exposure, we need to be aware of our public selves and the types of conversations we are having. Not everyone is going to like us; some may deeply dislike us for our mere existence or for what we've accomplished or didn't accomplish. Some may choose to connect because of what they may gain or take from you. Just be aware you will not know the intentions of everyone you encounter. Do the work required to tame your own insecurities so that each encounter is more in the moment and not reflective of something similar from the past. And if the beehive becomes a swarm, keep your focus on the folks who constitute your audience, tribe, fans, and friends.

Full Circle: Framing Your Story

What type of "bee" are
you when you network?

What are your networking
intentions and boundaries?

What types of networking
best serves your
business goals?

An *unresolved* past can
color *every situation*.

Fortune is a subjective
term that depends on both
your self-worth and how
you give of your time,
talents, and resources.

CHAPTER 17

Fortunes

Money Boot Camp

Growing up without money for school clothes or a second pair of shoes for sports, then eventually losing our home, gave me some strong limiting beliefs about money. I've had to rewrite my beliefs about money. I saw how long and hard both of my parents worked. If they weren't able to afford our family's basic needs, what chance did I have to be financially secure?

I believed that my destiny was a lifetime of struggling and falling short financially, just as my parents had. Either that or I'd have to work even longer and harder to have money. Thankfully, I've developed a more positive relationship with money and have learned to understand it better.

Money is simply energy that flows to us and from us. I've discovered that the more I give, without the expectation of being "paid back," the more riches flow back to me. It isn't magic but I've observed a universal law that we must give to receive.

But there's a huge difference between giving freely and earning pay. If we are giving with the expectation of receiving an income, we need to be intentional about affixing a price tag that reflects the value of our time, talents, wisdom, and energy. Getting clear on the motivation for my giving positively changed my relationship with money.

Money issues have also served to redirect my energy and reenergize my business. Each time money was sparse, I delved deeper into my creative resources and ended up learning skills I didn't know I needed. Each time, without fail, I came out of the situation stronger, with new ways for money to come into my business.

Scarcity came whenever I resisted change or doubted my ability to face that change. Sometimes it signaled that the direction in which my business was heading needed to be reviewed and corrected. This usually happened after I'd already been given plenty of opportunities to redirect.

The heavens have a way of saying, "Enough is enough," either by shutting off the money or shutting down the body. Either way, it's a clear indication that something has to change. Immediately.

"I Wanna Make a Million Dollars"

Our class exit project in design school was creating a book in which each student was depicted as a music legend. It included a photo of each classmate dressed as the music artist of their choice and a bio intertwining their design and production skills with the artist's personality. We drew names from a bowl and worked in teams to create one another's pages.

It was a small class, and my roommate and I just happened to draw one another's names. My roomie was portrayed as Madonna. I was the great Tina Turner because we both had legs that went on forever, plus a common yearning to make a million dollars. I took the headline for my project page from the lyrics of Tina Turner's hit song *Private Dancer*. This was the battle cry of my early career: "I wanna make a million dollars." I had no plan of action, just a large brushstroke of a dream to have a career that I loved while making lots of money doing graphic design work.

If I could time travel, I'd redo that headline—and rethink the big hair and mini skirt—but all that's sealed in time. I spent most of my career with a goal to "make a million dollars," all the while deeply believing I would never achieve it.

I've since redefined what making that million dollars means to me. But part of my dream was always about being paid well for doing good work for good people. It's a shame that I didn't believe I had the skills to be richly compensated. It pains me to reflect upon that.

How many times do we set financial goals and work hard toward reaching them without real plans for achieving success? We are actually sabotaging our dreams and short-circuiting the positive flow of energy that could come our way. I had my right foot pushed all the way down on the proverbial accelerator, my wheels pointed forward, while constantly tapping on the brakes with my left foot. That made my life dizzy and caused my business to move in fits and starts. I failed to gain forward traction for many, many years.

At the time, I didn't understand that my fantasy of making a million dollars revealed not only my aspirations but also my lack of self-worth. Over time and through personal and spiritual development, I've created a new relationship with money and no longer need that battle cry. Fortunately, while providing valuable creative and publication services, my team has generated millions of dollars into the firm. I now measure the success of my career and life in fortunes both seen and *unseen*.

Giving

Your business does not need to be super-profitable to give. In fact, I launched my business with a component of giving within the first few weeks. When I don't give, I feel my heart breaking. Giving fuels me personally.

If you ever had a personal block against creating wealth, giving with the intention to serve helps overcome it. There is nothing more satisfying than giving something of value to someone else without expectation or possibility of repayment.

The gift that my mentor and guide Yvonne gave me created a debt I could never repay. It created a drive in me to give back as much as I can to others. I know that no matter how much I give, it will never match the value of her teaching me how to transform my life. Because of this, I'm dedicated to a lifetime of service.

Our amazing *b2bTRIBE* magazine was created as a passion project. I'm wise enough to know that you don't start a business venture without it generating profit. But this project was not launched to generate profit. Not a penny. My goal was simply to break even. And what drove me was a sincere desire to share stories about the truth, beauty, diversity, and hardship of business ownership.

The magazine spotlighted over 600 local, small business owners and their companies, at no cost to them. My creative team planned and executed the photo shoots, wrote and edited the text, designed the gorgeous, full-color magazine pages, and then sent it to be printed and direct-mailed. My mission, beyond telling these unique stories, was to unify our community's business owners.

From a giving and connection standpoint, the magazine and its related public events were a stunning success. However, it took a great deal of focus and energy away from my business during a time when I needed to be fully present. And I learned that the small business owner community, for the most part, didn't much care about becoming unified. Most business owners were too entrenched in their own "stuff" to lift up their heads and notice what other owners were doing.

Although our efforts were applauded by local business associations and chambers, they weren't inclined to

Getting *clear* on the
motivation for my
giving *positively*
changed my *relationship*
with *money.*

collaborate with us. I was saddened by the lack of reciprocity. I had given to this local audience with the best intentions.

Nevertheless, the impact of *b2bTRIBE* magazine extended far and wide. We didn't receive referrals locally, but the magazine attracted positive attention nationally. As a direct result of this publication, we landed two large magazine accounts for national associations.

That was not part of my vision. Not at all. It served as an encouraging example of how any deed done with a pure heart can create beautiful consequences. And the timing and ultimate direction of what we put "out there" is ultimately out of our control.

Give to Grow

It's a new business model: providing value to your audience without trying to sell them something. If potential customers can experience, firsthand, the worth of what you've given them for free, they'll likely sign up to buy the high-end, customized services or products you offer. Make sure to attract them with several points of entry at different price points.

But please never ever expect recipients to buy simply because you gave them something for free—that breaks the flow of energy. It also destroys trust. Your gift will get their attention, and sales will come from having properly targeted your audience and offering them genuine value.

Full Circle: Framing Your Story

What are your beliefs about
how money flows into your
life? How does money
flow into your business?

In what ways do you give
to your community without
expecting a return?

How do you practice giving
as part your business
development strategy?

It's a new *business* model: *providing value* to your audience *without* trying to *sell them something*.

Flourishing as a business owner goes far beyond your profit and loss statement. To flourish you must also have intellectual, spiritual, and interpersonal fulfillment, as well as gratitude.

CHAPTER 18

Flourish

The Wisdom Gained through Practice

As a business owner, I'm constantly gathering knowledge. There was a time when I found myself focused on learning from several guides, mentors, programs, advisors, and mastermind groups. Accumulating information and advice on business development, leadership, and marketing was of no value to my firm until I'd applied and reapplied the knowledge. Without putting what was learned into practice, I became knowledge rich but experience poor. This contributes little to wisdom or the bottom line.

At some point on our business journeys, it's time to stop consuming knowledge like fear-filled information addicts and do something with it. As this new knowledge is put to the test, other ideas and approaches tend to show up. And eventually we gain true wisdom.

Gratitude

Cultivating gratitude for what's around us, who's around us, and what we do can changes our outlook on everything.

As I'm pulling the covers up to my chin at night, I fill my heart with gratitude for the lessons and the love the day has brought. This feels like a challenge after a stressful day. But that's when gratitude is even more important. After losing a large client, it's befitting to appreciate the clients I *do* have. After trying to figure out where the money is going to come from for payroll, it's befitting to be grateful for everything that *is* paid for.

I end most days by sending out these simple words to the Universe: "Thank you." Sometimes it's "thank you, thank you, thank you" in the form of a plea, but nonetheless, these words help shift my attitude to gratitude.

Spiritual Core

Learning to tune in to internal feelings and reactions to situations was a big step toward awareness of a life beyond what I consciously knew. Continuing to explore my spiritual core and seek deeper meaning in everything I do and every choice I make is an ongoing task. I do this by asking myself questions. Gaining awareness has helped me to ask myself better questions. And these often generate new questions.

If you have no idea what question to ask, start with why. Then with every answer, drill down further by asking why at least five more times:

Why did I react that way?
Why does it matter?
And why does that matter?
Why would that bother me?
Why?

Do this exercise quickly, so there's no time to change the conversation. It will likely reveal underlying topics that surprise you and give you new ideas to reflect upon. For example, through a series of questions, I discovered that my ego was protecting me by resisting change. It fought to maintain the

The *journey* of
"*accessing* our
spiritual *cores*" is
interchangeable with
"growing
our businesses."

status quo and save me from any discomfort or pain involved with change.

If a topic is too sensitive, get one of your guides to ask you the questions. Or get that friend who wants only the best for you and doesn't let you get away with anything. You know the one.

Becoming more self-aware and dropping our ego shields makes us more vulnerable. Along with that vulnerability comes a deeper level of self-honesty and the courage to discover more about ourselves. This courage helps us face our internal challenges and builds resilience for overcoming external challenges.

Building my spiritual core isn't about sitting on top of a mountain and looking down upon others. It's about becoming the best that I can be. The more I learn about my own capabilities, the more I see that we are all doing the best that we can with the knowledge and experiences that we have. When we know better, we do better. When we love ourselves more, we are more compassionate. When we understand more, we are more patient. When we learn more about ourselves, we are more accepting of those around us. That's why infusing spirituality into our business practices helps us make our processes more complete and more valuable.

The journey of "accessing our spiritual cores" is interchangeable with "growing our businesses." Both follow in the steps of what Joseph Campbell calls the "hero's journey." We can't bypass any of the steps—each reveals capabilities and aspects of ourselves never before realized.

Fulfillment

By my personal definition, "fulfillment" is the ultimate reward for a business well run and a life well lived. It was also supposed to be the main title of this chapter, not just a subhead. But the truth is, I couldn't write a chapter with that title. It suggested I create a blissful tale, complete with beautiful adjectives and inspiring scenes of success. This was my fear-induced thought: *What story can I possibly share about fulfillment after having exposed so many of my business failures and fears?*

Anyway, all the other chapters were written and rewritten four times. They had gone through both a structural edit and then a copy edit, but the chapter titled "Fulfillment" remained blank. The "Fear" chapter had given me angst too, but I understood dodging that one until the third rewrite. After all, who avoids fear better than me? But why, oh why, was "Fulfillment" so hard to write?

As it turns out, my roadblocks to writing about fulfillment provided both insights and further questions. Allow me to be vulnerable once again in sharing them. Perhaps they will ring true for you and your business.

Perfectionism: I've proven to myself that I can summarize a personal story of firsthand lessons learned and share it with honesty and vulnerability. However, as I was wrapping up writing this book, I wanted to tie the package with a pretty ribbon and bow. I wanted to offer a perfect payoff for the trials and tribulations of my business journey—something along the lines of bliss.

But what is the definition of "perfect"? How long is perfection supposed to last? And who gets to label something as perfect? And what are the criteria? All of us must decide what perfection looks like in our own businesses. And the truth is, if we look carefully, we will find blissfully perfect points throughout our journeys. There are times when everything falls into place and we celebrate a great outcome. However, the moment of perfection may be when the pieces come together and some don't fit, prompting a shift in attitude. Either way, the next phase begins in that moment.

People Pleasing: I want this book to hold great value for you; I want to please you, so you'll share it with other business owners. I want to bring you stories that save you time or hardship on your journey. And I want to give you emotional support and remind you that you're not alone. Finally, I want to prove that growing spiritually and making a profit as the owner of a heart-centered small business is more than a great vision; it's also doable. But what if I can't properly convey fulfillment, the ultimate end-game reward (beyond profitability), and you're displeased?

Fantasy: "Dream big," we're told. But without actionable plans, our dreams are merely fantasy. I wondered what actionable plans I was overlooking as I completed this book. How could I bring readers the greatest value and effectively wrap up these stories and lessons? I continued to stare at the screen with my blinking curser hovering under the word "fulfillment."

I procrastinated as long as I could and finally wrote my editor a note. I shared with her that I loved the structural and copy edits she was making but admitted that my inner critic was screaming about my inability to form a concise thought. I confessed that I'd lost my confidence to write the final chapters. My super-sweet and gentle human of an editor simply responded, "Tell your inner-critic to kindly shut the *F* word up."

After laughing out loud and cleaning up the tea I spewed, I knew what I needed to do. I would continue to write from an honest and transparent perspective. It's what I've done throughout this entire book, so why change now?

I created a workaround by making "fulfillment" a subhead to the new chapter. This downplays the end-goal aspect of fulfillment and better suits the business owner version of ultimate rewards.

The truth is, we entrepreneurs gain wisdom and satisfaction as we ride the roller coaster of business ownership. It goes beyond the numbers on our profit and loss sheets; it's the stories that those numbers tell. The "contributions" line item is about a heart fulfilled by generosity that goes beyond payroll and client care. That line item "profit" is about the joy of

The *truth* is,
we *entrepreneurs* gain
wisdom and *satisfaction* as
we ride the *roller coaster*
of *business* ownership.
It goes *beyond the numbers*
on our *profit* and loss sheets;
it's the *stories* that
those *numbers* tell.

providing highly valued goods and services. The "payroll" line item is about helping to support the livelihood of families in our communities.

Throughout the wild twists, turns, ups, downs, wins, and losses, we find fulfillment in the ride. It's not about the end. As entrepreneurs and business owners, the thought of the end terrifies us. We thrive on beginnings. We want the ride to reach new heights and to last forever.

Each night we lay down our heads, knowing or praying we'll do better tomorrow. Each month we either hit or miss our goals, having learned more than we ever thought we could in thirty days. Each year we hit metrics that constitute our end-of-year (EOY) financials, only to aim for higher percentages next year. EOY sales and profitability are the gauge for "how we're doing" and for landing loans or entry into certain networks and programs. And for the amount of money we can finally pay ourselves for our hard work.

Put the pressure of perfectionism and people-pleasing and fantasy aside. The goodness of the ride, the people, the work, the creativity, and the experiences gained—now that's true fulfillment!

Laughter, Fun, and Play

I work with my husband of over thirty years full-time, 24/7/365. How do we manage that tricky business and personal relationship?

First, we clearly defined our roles and responsibilities within the firm early on. We hired a coach to help us with what we didn't know we didn't know. We practice understanding and kindness. And we've learned how to negotiate the instances when our roles overlap and how to address challenges when they show up.

Secondly, we work hard at this business, and there are times when we go weeks without a day off. So we have to take breaks to be silly, watch a brainless show, and just have simple fun. And then we schedule time to step away from work and go on a jaunt to explore a nearby town for some bigger fun. We also formally claim our own alone time. He likes to illustrate in various media; I like to listen to soul-infused podcasts (thank you, Oprah and TED talks!) or write out my next dream project. We also plan some enjoyable trips and check off places around the globe we'd like to visit.

Thirdly, the habit that saves our business and our marriage is daily laughter. We often don't feel like laughing, and sometimes we laugh through the tears, but we consciously look for the humor or, at the very least, the absurdity in any given situation. With that daily dose of comedy, our relationship continues to flourish.

Full Circle: Framing Your Story

What if you could _____?
(Fill in the blank.)

What would you need to let
go of to make it happen?
What are the first steps?
Who would stop you?
What new opportunities
would this bring into your life?

How do you recognize the
people and things you're
grateful for every day?

Accumulated knowledge, experience, and wisdom fuse and become something even greater. Then it must be passed on, both for your own benefit and for others.

CHAPTER 19

Fusion

Your Knowledge, Their Lesson

A day comes in each of our lives when the knowledge we've gathered, the experiences we've absorbed, and the wisdom we've gained fuse and grow into something bigger than we can hold alone. The energy, the value of that knowledge must be released.

Perhaps it's not that the information is so vast or heavy; perhaps it simply no longer belongs only to us. It is now ready to educate, entertain, or enlighten those who need and are awaiting the knowledge. Holding it inside ourselves any longer would be selfish. Bonus: when you teach something, the knowledge takes on a different, fuller dimension for you.

Twice in my life I have felt that day arrive, and each time I wrote a book. Pouring the contents of your brain into a book is indeed an arduous process and at times an act of courage. But if I hadn't done it, you may not have learned that one thing that flipped your perspective or reframed a belief. The information was no longer just mine. It is now in your brain too. What knowledge can you package up and share to help shift the life of that one person who needs what you've learned?

The Drafts Reveal

Until completing my first book, I didn't fully understand why so many weird situations were showing up in my life. Writing that book helped me organize and reflect upon a lifetime of "happenings." By composing a timeline of events and retelling the stories, I was able to connect the dots. Often our lives don't make sense until we search for patterns of learning and discover how each hard lesson makes the next lesson a bit easier.

When speaking to others about writing my own books, people often comment, "Well, that should be easy since you help so many people publish their books."

Not true. My skills include clarifying the audience and infusing a client's passion, personality, and strategy into their book to add value to their platform and business. Then I have our team package it all up with a well-designed, marketable cover and targeted interior. But writing? That's not my strength.

Like most of my clients, I use written communications fairly effectively in my work, but I don't write at a professional level, at all. A good writing coach, structural editor, copy editor, and proofreader are invaluable to a manuscript. Writing for publication is an extensive process.

From Brain to Emotions to Paper

For me, it began in June 2017 when I had a dream about the outline of this book. I jumped out of bed at 2:00 a.m. to write it down. As the theme developed, the outline became a table of contents, which changed and was reorganized at least six times.

My first two manuscripts were basically journal-like entries and mind dumps. Writing candidly about my journey exposed emotions and unresolved conflicts I needed to work through. The manuscript was totally rewritten three times prior to sending it to my structural editor.

Often our
lives don't *make sense*
until we *search*
for *patterns* of learning
and *discover* how each
hard *lesson* makes
the *next* lesson
a bit easier.

Once she completed an editorial analysis of my manuscript, I rewrote it a fourth time. Sections were changed to consolidate chapters, and several were eliminated altogether. Honestly, it wasn't a manuscript until the fourth round. Prior rounds were rough drafts.

After the fourth rewrite, it was time for the structural edit. Concepts that popped up in several chapters were moved, merged, and streamlined. Several more chapters were removed or reorganized. Round five of the manuscript then went through the first copy-edit stage. I approved those edits and then sat on the manuscript for two months. There was a block; it wasn't the right time to complete this book or to promote it. Then we landed several public clients who were ready to publish their books, and my firm and I needed to give all of our attention to those high-profile projects. I used that time to select and invite a peer group to read and comment on the manuscript. Those peers included some people I felt would love the book as it was and some who were out of the target audience and would have strong opinions. They did not disappoint. Each comment and suggestion helped to take this book to yet another level of value for you, the reader.

The writing and editing process requires humbling, patient, and focused work. It stretched my memory, concentration, and skill. And in true form and fashion, I challenged each editor as we completed this manuscript. Is it perfect? Not at all. Is it of great value to the reader? Is it?

When *you know* who your *audience is*, you'll know there's *someone* out there *awaiting your book*.

After the manuscript was "done," the fun of production began, and I was back in my comfort zone. My team designed several covers, which took my vision beyond what I imagined, and the inside pages became their own work of art. After a final proofread before printing, we finally reached the marketing and promotion stage.

The process can be compared to methodically launching an intentional business, writing a business plan, and developing branding and marketing. Writing and publishing a book is, in fact, an entrepreneurial process. A custom book allows you to share your unique perspective and knowledge with your targeted audience, and it breaks through the clutter of social media, email communications, and streamed broadcasts.

Start Writing!

What knowledge have you accumulated? What story do you have to tell? How can you share that story to fuel your platform and best serve your audience? It's noble to want to help one mentee or one client at a time. But why limit your vision? Why not go for a moon-shot goal of service to a targeted, widespread audience of readers? Start writing with purpose and get that book professionally published and out of your head! We've got a few free resources to help you at SPARKpublications.com/books.

So now you know the secret process. It isn't magic. It may seem like folks can pop a book out in two months, but it's more likely they have learned not to share their progress publicly. When well-meaning people ask, "When will your book be available?" and you're thinking you may never finish, it's like when your parents ask, "When are you going to give us a grandchild?" Who needs that kind of pressure? Consider keeping quiet about your book until after you write your crappy first draft, rewrite it, and rewrite it again. Then you can share with a few folks because at that stage you're going to need some encouragement.

As you begin, if you're writing on your own, do build your support system of talent and cheerleaders. And whatever you do, remember your audience. When you know who your audience is, you'll know there's someone out there awaiting your book.

Full Circle: Framing Your Story

What knowledge have you accumulated that is ready to share with an audience?

How can you share your knowledge in a way that fuels your business?

What steps do you need to take to make that happen?

A *day* comes in each
of *our lives* when
the *knowledge* we've
gathered, the *experiences*
we've *absorbed,* and the
wisdom we've *gained* fuse
and *grow* into something
bigger than
we can *hold* alone.

Mentoring and letting someone "pick your brain" are very different things. Do the former. Don't fall for the latter.

CHAPTER 20

Footnotes

A Few Final Insights

A large number of lessons and stories were omitted from this book. I've included only those I think may be most valuable to you in strengthening your business. Although each of the following nuggets of experience could have a book dedicated to them, I'll shine a tiny spotlight on them in this one.

Mentoring

If we "made it on our own," it's because we didn't know how to ask for help. In addition to the blessing of having amazing guides, I've had the privilege of learning from valuable mentors. Joan Z. taught me to be unapologetic about loving to work and owning a business. Elizabeth M. showed me how to be a gracious networking queen. In his no-holds-barred yet kind way, Chris L. gave me sound sales-management strategies. Matthew B. shook me out of promotion mode to take a value-focused position. Jennifer M. showed me what faithful support looks like as a mentor. My peer group advisory mentors from NAWBO and 10KSB Charlotte MasterMind groups provided encouragement and introduction as we rolled up our sleeves and took turns in the hot seat. I am truly grateful for their generous service.

As I shared in the previous chapter, the knowledge and lessons we accumulate as we grow our businesses may be valuable to others who are considering entrepreneurship, just starting out, or taking their businesses through uncharted territories. If you see someone struggling or muddling through, invite them for a conversation. Share the story about how you handled a similar aspect of your business journey and encourage them to ask questions.

I abhor the question, "Can I pick your brain?" If someone asks me that, I let them know my brain-picking fee is $500 per hour at my office. Mentoring is not a meeting where you dole out your hard-earned knowledge to someone who wants to do what you do. Mentoring is a long-term relationship in which you build trust and help someone with your connections and experience.

We gain skills and confidence as mentees; however, there is even more to be gained as a mentor. Consider taking time to mentor. I recommend enrolling in a formal program to learn processes that will be most valuable to you and your future mentee.

The Business of Family

The three essentials for working with family members in your business are boundaries, job descriptions, and respect. Each must be clearly defined (no gray areas!), and most important, everyone needs to be aware of them (in writing with their signatures on each page).

The role of family is critical during the highs and lows of business. I've watched the two people I love most in this world work harder than anyone should have to during our tough times.

Non-related employees may perceive there are perks for family members, but I work hard to create an even playing field for all employees. When we hit hard financial times, I had to cut expenses so that non-related employees' salaries wouldn't be affected. That meant cutting my husband's salary and my own salary and draw. I also asked my daughter to reduce her hours and work a second job at a noncompeting business.

We've worked many, many weekends, late nights, and holidays to finish projects or to clean, organize, perform maintenance tasks, and upgrade systems. I look forward to a future where I can offer my family the perks they deserve for the non-paid time and limitless passion they've invested into the firm.

It's impossible to overstate how dedicated my husband has been to me throughout my business and life journey. He could work at larger companies (and has had offers) for double his current salary. He loves the work we do, yet he's made it clear that the reason he works so hard is to help me reach my dreams and to spend time together. Trying to explain how someone like me has earned such selfless love renders me speechless.

In earlier chapters, I shared the importance and value of my father's business journey to my own, but I haven't mentioned much about my mother's role in my life. My mother was the one behind the scenes, sweeping up the wreckage of each entrepreneurial ending, feeding us, being strict with us, and working labor-intensive jobs for low salaries to keep our family going. She was steadfast and loyal and didn't get to see her own dream come true until she turned seventy-six. She and I were estranged for about eleven years as I made my way through becoming an adult. In hindsight, I could have handled things so much better, but unfortunately, wisdom usually comes in hindsight. We reconnected a number of years ago and now talk on the phone for about an hour every weekend.

After the rough draft of this book, I realized I kept my family's story as separate from my business story. I then chose to publicly share my family's role in building my firm. I shared my passionate story within a nomination for a *Charlotte Business Journal* award application. We became a finalist, and then at the awards ceremony at the Ritz-Carlton, we were announced as winner of the 2018 First-Generation Family Business of the Year. It was an amazing way to celebrate my family's foundational impact on my business.

The person in my family I'm most proud of is my sister. She retired early from her corporate career and stepped into her husband's small business. My sister more than quadrupled the business, its staff, clients, and processes.

Our family's entrepreneurial history may end with my sister and me. Only time will tell. But I believe the good work that she and I have done for our families, communities, and employees has begun to heal our ancestral wounds. From a spiritual standpoint, it's pretty awesome to be entrenched in life's purpose and mission. And that, dear readers, is deep fulfillment.

Flow

There's a great flow to our world. But at times we may feel out of flow, when everything seems too difficult. I've learned that these are stages in both life and business. In my personal life and in my business, I've hit inflection points that I now realize let me know it was time to do something new. What's worked before will no longer be the way to do "it" anymore. Every market and industry is changing, and we need to stay current on consumer and client needs and requests. No, it's not easy, and yes, not keeping up shuts businesses down. Yes, we are going to have to change, and many will resist and want to keep things as they were. We all need to develop something new with deeper value for our clients, all while keeping love, kindness, and compassion as part of the change. And when that timing "block" happens, it isn't necessarily a sign to stop; it may

And *when* that timing
"block" *happens,*
it isn't necessarily
a *sign* to stop;
it may *simply* be
happening to *slow* us
down to *better* assess a
next step or *resource.*

simply be happening to slow us down to better assess a next step or resource.

We've done our research, lined up our resources, empowered our teams, and launched our awareness campaigns. Our mindset is right, and the time is now. We have to do the work, physically, mentally, emotionally, and spiritually, as we put the processes in place. Then all of a sudden, it's all in "flow mode," and it is beautiful. Someone will inadvertently say you're an overnight success. Celebrate that moment, then keep on flowing.

Failing Forward

We'd acquired thousands of subscribers to *b2bTRIBE* magazine, most of them local entrepreneurs. One of the hardest things about being the magazine's publisher was following up with business owners when their emails bounced back. Sadly, within the three years that our magazine was published, forty-eight of our participating small business owners in the Charlotte area closed their doors. I felt every single closure as a death of someone's livelihood and dream. This heartbreaking tale highlights the importance of building a personal support team of cheerleaders, mentors, and guides to reduce the chances of losing your business.

The fact is, as a business owner or entrepreneur, you are going to mess up. Sometimes you're going to mess up so hard that you don't think there's a way out. If you're taking risks, failure is, at some point, inevitable; all your decisions and actions won't be winners. You may lose a great deal of money or financially and emotionally hurt people for whom you're responsible or who care for you.

Some mistakes and failures can't be fixed. But the secret to moving on is adjusting your mindset and attitude, which allows you to move forward one minute, then one hour, then one day at a time. After a business disaster, it's critical that you find the courage to be a strong creator, and a strong leader, by changing

The fact is, *as a business owner* or entrepreneur,

you are going to mess up.

Sometimes *you're* going to *mess up so hard* that you *don't think* there's *a way out.* If you're *taking risks*, failure is, at some point, inevitable; all your *decisions* and *actions* won't *be winners.*

your perspective of the current circumstances. Even when you can't fix the situation, you can make amends and "do right" by repaying money owed and extending personal apologies. Develop a plan to do so. And accept the fact that some people may never forgive you. They don't owe you that.

Facing our screw-ups is never easy. Believe me—I know. Dealing with the aftermath of our mistakes may initially take more energy and courage than we think we have. But here's my suggestion: pay your debts and dues, learn the lessons, forgive yourself, and then move forward. Don't waste the experience; do better next time. Learn how to fail faster and smarter.

Forgive

The first person you'll need to forgive after the dust settles is yourself. So you missed the sign, the message, or the gigantic skywriting. You made a bad call and a really poor selection, purchase, hire, or partnership. You can choose to beat yourself up for years to come or to forgive yourself and move forward. Again, as Norman Lear says, "Over and next." And as my dad constantly reminds me, "The past is the past." Yes, that's a difficult message to hear in the midst of the muck. But we can't move forward if we're burdened down with ourselves as our own biggest punishers. There are plenty of others who will do the punishing for us. You'll at some point need to forgive them as well. Be kind to yourself, do the next thing right (for the right reasons), keep moving forward, and forgive yourself.

Festivities

We spend a great deal of time focusing, obsessing, and reflecting on what went wrong, the opportunities we missed, the mistakes and failures we contributed to. But you wouldn't be where you are today without some good wins, successful decisions, and right moves. Think of all the processes created, the happy clients, the beautiful check, and the job well done. Give yourself a pat on the back and a cheer, "Yay me!" Treat your team, thank your clients, and practice some deep gratitude for all the little and big things that went well to get you to where you are. Celebrate!

Fanning the Flame

If you don't like your business story, start a new chapter. Then keep adding chapters until you finally write your new story, your new book, your new life. Your past will always be "there." You now have a new and improved story, a new and improved way of bringing your past lessons into your business and your life. All are creating a stronger, healthier, happier vision.

Don't know where to start? Begin by identifying exactly what you don't like about your current business. How would changing just that one aspect begin to change your business and your personal life? What would your new version look like, and how would you feel? Allow yourself to imagine being immersed in this modified vision as if you're already living it (finally a professional reason to daydream!). Then determine what actions you'll need to take to make this vision a reality. Then take multiple actions that support your new dream, your new vision.

Remember that you'll be putting your past behind you, but the lessons it offered go forward as part of your new story. If not, you'll probably find yourself revisiting those same hard-earned lessons in the future.

Growing or changing your business is a process. It will not happen overnight. However, your attitude, beliefs, and mental contracts can change in an instant. It's my hope that the lessons I've shared about my *F* words journey will help you learn from my mistakes. And finally, my entrepreneurial friend, please know that you're never alone on this crazy roller-coaster ride. Do more than just hang on.

You've got this!

Full Circle: Framing Your Story

How can you give of your
time as a mentor? And who
would most benefit from
your questions and answers?

When was the last time
you felt like all was going
well and you were in flow?
Can you replicate how
you got to that point?

What story would you
share to fuel the world
with your knowledge?

You wouldn't be
where *you* are today
without *some*
good *wins,* successful
decisions, and
right moves.

A farewell is a "goodbye for now" that leads to the next chapter of your next great thing.

CHAPTER 21

Farewell

Our SPARK Shines On

Throughout this book, I've referred to SPARK Publications as "my firm," "my company," or "my business." That was intentional. I didn't want my company's name to pull you away from seeing yourself or your own company in the story. I was forgoing promotion to help keep you focused. Because my business has been the main catalyst for my personal, professional, and spiritual growth, it's time for me to brag a bit about my beloved SPARK Publications.

SPARK Publications designs custom magazines, catalogs, and custom books. These publications are produced for use on a variety of platforms, including print, digital, online, and interactive. We also produce custom content, which ranges from creative infographics to creative copy to custom photo illustrations.

I've learned countless lessons while developing a core team of extraordinary professionals. Our team is called the SPARKlers because, well, we're sparkly, and we always add a creative spark to our clients' publications and projects.

For over twenty years, we've been privileged to work with independent publishers, corporate communications departments, national associations, universities, and business owners. Our mission is to tell each client's brand story with the purpose of helping them grow, entertain, or educate their target audience.

If you know someone who needs effective layout and creative design for their magazine or someone who wants to publish a beautifully customized book or catalog (you perhaps?), please send them to SPARKpublications.com. Direct introductions can be emailed to us at info@SPARKpublications.com. We'd love to see if we can be of service.

Next Chapter

This book took me a full year to write, counting from the moment I woke up in the middle of the night with the concept to the completion of the final paragraph. As I wrote each section, chapter, and story, I *unlived* the emotional attachments to each experience. My biggest lesson in writing this book was discovering the extent to which doubt and fear have influenced me in creating failures within my business. Sharing those failures used to debilitate me. And yes, they still knock the wind out of me for a bit, but then I can breathe even deeper, which creates a powerful new fuel.

Through writing this book I realized I am not immune to failure. I'm not going to lie and tell you I welcome it. However, failure lets me know that I've pushed my boundaries into a personal unknown. Sometimes it was an unknown I've created through doubt, lack of knowledge, or bad timing. Writing became a device for clarifying and redefining my business journey of failures and successes. Now this book will become the tool that launches me into my next uncharted territory.

The introvert in me so wanted to remain secluded in my happy, tiny, life bubble. However, a stirring deep inside me said to shine a spotlight on everything I've gone through, the wisdom I've learned, and the gifts I've developed—they are no longer for me to keep in my small bubble.

My next chapter is about sharing these lessons on my new path with you. I don't yet know what this path looks like or what it will lead to. And for the first time in my life, I am choosing to work with the Universe, instead of trying to micromanage it.

I look forward to meeting you at a near future workshop, conference, or across the airwaves. I hope in reading *Fabulous F Words of Business Ownership* you have gained new tools to better network, build your culture, break through doubt, and nurture your business with love and wisdom. And perhaps, you've redefined a few choice words to fuel your small business.

To a Fabulous Forever!

Fabi

P.S. – I'd love to hear from you about how you've redefined your choice words to fuel your business and about your favorite *F* words of business ownership.
Post on facebook.com/FabiPreslar
or post on FabiPreslar.com.

Let's stay connected!

Fabulous F Words of Business Ownership

A *stirring* deep *inside* me said to shine a *spotlight* on everything I've gone through, the *wisdom* I've *learned,* and the *gifts* I've *developed*— they are *no longer* for me *to keep* in *my small bubble.*

With Gratitude

There are so many amazing people to thank for so many things throughout my career. I truly appreciate the favor and grace.

As independent as I have been my entire life, I didn't begin to fully live until I allowed people to help me. Every single person I've interacted with has beautifully shaped my life. For brevity I want to take this quick note to share my gratitude for the small tribe who helped to make this book project come to life.

Thank you

Wendy G. for being a wonderful guide, interpreter, and friend while helping me sort out my crappy first drafts of emotion-filled, journal-like musings. Your talent helped me to create the structure for this book.

Melisa G. for the talented editing on my many, many rewrites, extracting the pull quotes, and writing the summaries.

It is difficult and indeed takes courage to share your raw and very personal work with peers, friends, and mentors. I am deeply grateful for the hours and passionate comments, critiques, and suggestions made by an amazing team of peer reviewers. You all challenged me more than you'll ever know.

Your honesty and perspectives made this book more valuable for the reader: Anne L., Chris D., Christine M., Carlos S., Carla R., Debbie P., Jacky C., JP W., Julie B., Kim B., Matt B., Melody M., Mike L., Nathalie C., and Sherré D.

I am consistently blown away by the care, love, and creativity of the SPARK Publications team. I truly appreciate their great questions and their talents in executing my vision so beautifully with words, cover, interior, webpage, and social media design, as well as with the marketing, promotion, and publicity for every aspect of this book. I am beyond proud of the work they create for our clients and am delighted for the work we've completed together on this project. A SPARKly sprinkle of gratitude to the SPARKlers: Jim D., Genna H., Melisa G., Arden M., Bonnie D., and of course, hourly gratitude to Larry and Sofi Preslar.

I'm Forever Grateful!

ABOUT THE AUTHOR

Fabi Preslar is owner and president of SPARK Publications, an independent publishing and creative firm specializing in custom design for magazines, catalogs, and books for print, digital, and interactive formats. Her clients include national associations, independent publishers, and professionals who share their knowledge to educate and enlighten their audiences. The firm was launched in 1998.

Fabi has pushed her personal boundaries to accomplish much more than she ever thought possible. This included being celebrated as the 2018 First-Generation Family Business of the Year by the *Charlotte Business Journal*, the 2017 Women Business Owner of the Year by the National Association of Women Business Owners (NAWBO)–Charlotte Chapter, and 2015 Marketer of the Year by the Business Marketing Association of the Carolinas. She also received the Career Mastered National Leadership Award and has twice been celebrated as one of *Mecklenburg Times'* 50 Most Influential Women. She serves as a mentor and advisor with the Women's Inter-Cultural Exchange and independently mentors several women small business owners. She's also publisher of *b2bTRIBE* magazine and author of *On Heaven's Couch: My Journey with a Masterful Mentor.* Her second book, *Fabulous F Words of Business Ownership,* shares her strong entrepreneurial passion as well as her journey through fear, failure, faith, and a variety of other *F* words along the way as an introverted business owner. Her days are surrounded by her firm's creativity and a very talented team, which includes her husband of thirty-two years, Larry, and their daughter, Sofi. Visit SPARKpublications.com to learn more.

To hire Fabi as a speaker, consultant or for an interview go to FabiPreslar.com

YOUR NEXT ACTION TO-DO'S:

☐ Download the feedback grid (mentioned on page 125) at FabiPreslar.com/resources.

☐ Pick a chapter each week and go back to the end of that chapter to deeply answer each question (several times).

☐ Send a business owner to FabiPreslar.com, so they can order their own copy of *Fabulous F Words of Business Ownership*.

☐ Refer Fabi to speak at your meeting, conference, or association events.

☐ Start writing down your knowledge and fusing your story. Connect with SPARKpublications.com to publish your next book, magazine, or catalog.

☐ List your top three action steps to take your business to the next awesome level:
-
-
-

Visit FabiPreslar.com
to read *F* word stories from
other business owners, share
your own, download resources,
and connect with Fabi Preslar.

To get your book independently
and custom published, start
at SPARKpublications.com

Fabulous F WORDS™ OF BUSINESS OWNERSHIP

CPSIA information can be obtained
at www.ICGtesting.com
Printed in the USA
LVHW031320150320
650084LV00010B/898